Archetypes
of
Women in Scripture

D1296023

Craig Ballard Millett

IN GOD'S IMAGE

San Diego, California

LuraMedia ™

Cover Design, Carol Jeanotilla, Denver, CO
Printed on recycled paper.

LuraMedia, Inc.
7060 Miramar Road, Suite 104
San Diego, CA 92121

Library of Congress Cataloging-in-Publication Data
Millett, Craig Ballard,
    In God's image : archetypes of women in scripture / by Craig
Ballard Millett.
        p.   cm.
    Includes bibliographical references.
    ISBN 0-931055-77-6
    1. Women in the Bible. 2. Feminist theology. 3. Archetype
(Psychology) I. Title.
BS575.M53   1991
220.6'082—dc20
                                                    90-20578
                                                    CIP

Grateful acknowledgment is made to the following copyright holders for permission to use their copyrighted material:

Princeton University Press for the quotation from *The Collected Works of C. G. Jung,* trans. R. F. C. Hull, Bollingen Series 20, Vol. 2: *Experimental Researches,* copyright © 1973 by Princeton University Press.

Scripture quotations are from the New Revised Standard Version of the Bible, copyright 1989 by the Division of Christian Education of the National Council of the Churches of Christ in the USA and used by permission.

Contents

Acknowledgments

I would like to acknowledge help in the writing of this book from many sources throughout my life. I thank my parents for giving me a name that would cause me to search for a deeper identity. I thank my teachers and mentors throughout the years who have believed in my capabilities more than I. I thank the many women who have broken free of social stereotypes and have exemplified power, justice, intelligence, strength, and integrity. I thank the three beautiful young women who happen to be my daughters: Aliicia, Laura, and Jeanne. Our road together has not always been easy, but watching them grow up into complete and caring human beings has been and will always be one of the greatest joys of my life. And, most especially, I thank my husband, the Reverend Dr. David Waite Yohn, for loving me as the person I was created to be. Finally, I offer my praise and thanks to the God in whose image I am formed.

PART
ONE

INTRODUCTION

As a female, I have struggled almost from birth with having a man's name. I am always asked to repeat it, as if I had made a mistake. "Craig? No, dear, what is *your* name?" And then the inevitable comment comes: "Your parents must have wanted a boy." Teachers always made similar comments the first day of class, thus singling me out as someone who was a little "different." Mail often comes addressed to me as "Mr." and banks insist that I reendorse my own checks. Workshop and seminar registrars register me with the male participants. I am continuously left off mailings for women's events. Only in middle age have I begun to sort out all of the mixed messages and conflicting feelings that I have had about my own identity as a woman.

These past ten years, particularly, have been ones of intense personal and spiritual upheaval. In dealing with these traumas, I have sought help from therapists, counselors, and pastors, most of whom have been enormously helpful. I have talked to men and women individually and in groups. I have earned two graduate degrees, immersed myself in feminist literature, and taught seminary courses in the psychology and spirituality of women.

Through it all, I have been impressed with the number of other women who were asking the same questions as I. In the beginning, I clung to my Bible like my children used to cling to their security blankets, even while despairing of the sexism rampant between its covers. Soon, however, the graduate studies in theology and psychology made reading Scripture feel like salt was being rubbed into my freshly opened feminist wounds. Therefore, like many of my sisters, I found myself turning from my faith tradition to discover the wonderful affirmation and celebration of the feminine found in ancient matrifocal societies and religions of times long past. It was a wonderful release and respite. But after a while, it became apparent to me that it was not enough. I also needed the powerful symbols of my church.

Psychologically, I found in the Goddesses the affirmation and self-worth as a woman that I lacked. Spiritually, however, I needed something other than my own wholeness to worship. And so, out of my own personal dilemma, I began to try to put the two together. In writing a sermon for Advent a few years ago, I began to notice how many of our most sacred symbols have a decidedly feminine nature. For example, I began to appreciate the church year as a way to spiritually experience the truth of the ancient Great Round. I viewed baptism less from a theological point of view and more from my perspective as a mother, which drew me into a much more visceral comprehension of this miraculous symbol of birth and re-birth. As a woman clergy, I administered the Eucharist as a woman offers nourishing food at her biological family's table.

As I allowed my sensibilities as a woman to reinterpret my faith in these ways, much of what I had thought was a hopelessly patriarchal religion began to take on a much deeper and more profound significance. And so, painfully and tenderly, I have returned to the Scriptures, to tiptoe between the nettles of misogyny and to discover what is, to me, a golden thread that speaks specifically to the worth of women's experience. The following pages, therefore, have a very intentional purpose: to help others along the same journey that I am on and to share with them the possibility that we can integrate the teachings of psychology, the strength of the Goddesses, and the power of our faith in celebration of the women that we are.

Craig Ballard Millett
1990

CHAPTER ONE

Women, Psychology, and Scripture

Or what woman having ten silver coins, if she loses one of them, does not light a lamp, sweep the house, and search carefully until she finds it? When she has found it, she calls together her friends and neighbors, saying, "Rejoice with me, for I have found the coin that I had lost" (Luke 15:8-9).

The woman in this parable is representative of God seeking a lost soul. She looks everywhere she can think of and then throws a big party in celebration when she finds the one that was lost. It is a wonderful image of God. God is a homemaker hunting under the furniture, looking for us. God is not going to allow even one of us to be lost. And, God likes to throw parties!

The parable is also an appropriate image of women who are searching for a lost part of themselves. We instinctively know that something very precious is missing, and we look everywhere we can think of to find it. Too often we go beyond our own boundaries and seek it from others, not understanding that it has been hidden in one of our own dark corners all the time. We simply have not seen it.

One of the most pressing quests of every person is the search for personal identity. For women, it is a particularly intricate task because there are so many forces from outside ourselves telling us what the answer should be. It is often difficult to block these voices and to answer the question according to our own intuitive awareness. Moreover, it is only recently that most of us have felt that we had that option or that right. In the past twenty years, however, significant gains have been made in women's appreciation and affirmation of our own reality. Writers such as Carol Gilligan, Anne Wilson Schaef, Susan Brownmiller, and Jean Baker Miller have joined the voices of Simone de Beauvoir and Betty Friedan in celebrating strengths and skills of women in new and exciting ways. They have also been painfully articulate in pointing out the damage done to women over the years by the patriarchal social order of which we are part, including the psychological acceptance of the male personality as the norm.

Feminist theologians such as Mary Daly, Rosemary Radford Ruether, Phyllis Trible, Elisabeth Schussler Fiorenza, and Virginia Ramey Mollenkott have joined the psychologists and social critics in their condemnation of patriarchy by articulating the sexism of the churches and of the Judeo-Christian tradition. They have then used their gifts of scholarship to celebrate women's reality as an integral part of God's creation and to affirm for once and for all our appointed place in the divine image.

Careful biblical exegesis has now proven without doubt that the creation narratives in Genesis refer to an androgynous Creator who includes both genders while being beyond all gender identification. The human creatures formed in the image of this androgynous God are male and female, representing the two realities of the divine. However, much of the rest of Scripture is not as clear. Masculine images of God vastly outnumber feminine although, like the one Lukan parable above, they can be found. It is partly a problem of language, of not having an androgynous pronoun to include the fullness of the divinity, but even more it reflects the extremely patriarchal culture within which the Bible was written.

The emphasis on a male God, however, has become more and

more problematic to women who are trying to celebrate their worth as articulated by the psychologists. The sexist language, images, and hierarchical structures of the churches sound more and more exclusive. Women try to find themselves in the image of the Father but often cannot. Many have left their faith traditions, reluctantly and painfully, because the churches would not celebrate with them the lost sense of worth that psychology has helped them find.

Insights in Archetypes

Jungian feminists, in naming attributes of women that were at least once considered to be holy, have led many of us back to the ancient Goddess. Anthropologists tell us that worship of her reality was nearly universal for at least 25,000 years before Abram and Sarai left Haran for the promised land. She is therefore much older than the Judeo-Christian God. Jean Shinoda Bolen and other Jungians have, without concerning themselves with the religious overtones, helped to identify the positive and negative attributes and powers of the Goddess in hopes of helping women find the same realities in themselves.

In psychological language, or at least in Jungian language, the Goddess represents archetypal woman, the image of what it means to be universal "woman." An archetype is a universal way of perceiving a given set of images. For example, the archetypal journey is one with a hero or heroine who must survive unknown dangers and challenges, often aided by strange people or talking animals and who always conquers all odds in the end and usually ends up as either the new king or the bride of one.

Archetypes are the language of fairy tales and legends and often our own dreams. They generate enormous psychic energy because they are recognizable to the depths of our soul. We all know the wise old woman or the wicked witch, the divine child or the royal marriage, even though we have probably never witnessed any of them. Archetypes are ageless and universal. However, their images may vary. An obvious example would be that of the archetypal good mother. Each of us will image her in a different way, according to our own memory, our nationality, and our race. However, the universality of the archetype itself will be the same regardless of who we are or where we are from. The good mother still means, among other things, gestation, birth, nurturing, compassion, food, generosity, self-sacrifice, warmth, security, and love. So it is with all of the archetypes. Their images may vary, but their basic reality will always remain the same.

Ancient Goddesses

The Goddess of ancient times was the archetypal image of all women, motherhood being one of her most powerful attributes — but not the only one. She was creator, warrior, one who gave advice, one who was loyal and persistent, intelligent and strong. There was no sense of the weakness or passivity of stereotypical femininity that is so pervasive today. The Goddess ruled both life and death since death was accepted as a natural part of the life cycle. Early people who lived close to the earth knew that spring never came without winter, and that new life always rose out of decay. This sense of the Great Round of life and death was one of the Goddess' most potent images. Her symbol was often the serpent, the only animal that shed its skin while still alive and that could form the circle, the symbol of eternal life.

In time, however, warrior tribes with male deities overcame her people, and she was replaced by male gods. She became fragmented into various lesser Goddesses in order to weaken her original power. Each one of these then had a myth built around her that explained who she was according to what had happened to her. In these stories, we can recognize universal experiences of women. Greece and Rome, for example, had Goddesses of war and of home. There was the mother Goddess and the wife of the god-king. There was a Goddess of wisdom and many more. These Goddesses, however, were all subject to male gods and were often abused and victimized by them.

Jean Shinoda Bolen, in the bestselling book *Goddesses in Everywoman*, identifies seven of these Goddesses as the major images or archetypes of women's reality. As a Jungian analyst, she recognized that her clients were living out of different sets of perspectives, attitudes, priorities, and values. Some women were independent; others defined themselves through their relationships.

Some were comfortable with the structures of today's society; others were feminists who wanted radical change. Some identified themselves firmly as wives and mothers; others were very happy as singles. She began to identify them with various Greek Goddesses, and their differences began to make sense.

In her book, Bolen separates what she calls the three virgin (or independent) Goddesses from the three vulnerable (or relational) ones. She then adds a seventh, an "alchemical" Goddess, who provides energy to the others for change and growth. Bolen notes that most women live out the pattern of at least one of these archetypes. She suggests that psychological integration means utilizing the personalities of at least one of the virgin Goddesses and one of the vulnerable ones plus the final energy of the seventh. A woman who is totally virginal or too independent might miss out on the joys of relationship and a woman who is too vulnerable is in danger of becoming victimized. The seventh archetype is needed by all to switch from one to another as it becomes necessary.

Many women have found the Goddesses to be very helpful as images to whom they can relate. Psychologically, they provide representations of a woman's inner being that enable her to know herself and to expand her capabilities beyond their present state. Others were uncomfortable with the implications of Goddesses in terms of their faith. They can neither equate Zeus with God nor worship these oft-victimized women. Yet they feel pulled between their own religious heritage and their psychological needs. On the one hand, they feel a need to identify with womanly reality, and on the other, they want to be included among the children of God. They wonder whether they were created in the divine image of the Goddess or the divine image of God.

Finding the Feminine in Scripture

What if, for a moment, we could break out of the analytical and divisive mentality of either/or thinking and try to embrace a perspective that includes both/and? It may be that we are created in the image of both God and Goddess. In fact, it may well be that the source of life and light and love that we call God also includes all of the attributes of the earlier deity. We may, hopefully, be at a place in our own development where we can look back to the strengths of matriarchal religion and to the strengths of the patriarchal God and combine the best of both.

The problem we face in tying a gender to God may be more in our inability to conceptualize than it is in the reality of the One we worship. To use a strictly anthropomorphic image, living creatures need both the sperm of a father and the ova of a mother for conception to occur. Why should our spiritual self be any different? Scripture, as patriarchal as it is, contains a remarkable number of divine images that are decidedly more female than male. God conceives and gives birth, mothers her children, shows maternal compassion for the weak and sick and oppressed, offers rebirth in the divine amniotic waters of baptism, and feeds her family with the eucharistic meal. All of these images and more are traces of the Goddess in God, of the maternal divinity as well as the paternal one.

Our Roman Catholic and Orthodox sisters have been able to retain reverence for at least part of her reality in the person of Jesus' mother, Mary. Protestants, however, have been left bereft of any female presence in their faith at all. Both/and thinking would allow us to expand our faith and our worship, allowing the Goddess, or archetypal woman, to take her part in the Deity that we honor. She is already within our soul, held deep within the collective unconscious of all people — a memory trace of thousands of years ago. Perhaps the visceral, fearful reaction to her return is due to this very fact. If she did not threaten the relatively new domination of the male, she would probably be ignored. As it is, we can now perhaps begin to include her in our thinking as we celebrate with the theologians the newly affirmed place of women in the holy image of God.

Biblical Archetypes

Our next task, then, takes us back to psychology. If the archetypal realities that Bolen identified in her clients are universal, then there will be many images other than the Goddesses to whom we can relate. And since we are looking for representatives of the feminine side of the imago Dei in such a way that we do not have to jettison the valuable aspects of our own faith tradition, the logical place to begin is in Scripture. In fact, naming scriptural women as arche-typal images provides a much more wholesome and integrated picture of who we are.

Rather than identifying with victimized fragments of a once powerful Goddess, we can find mortal women who are called by God to be whole and complete people. Identifying with these women, we can accept our place as equal inheritors of divine energy or grace. As females created in God's image, we become, with them, true daughters of the female God.

The same seven archetypes of women's reality that Bolen identified with the Greco-Roman Goddesses we will find in scrip-tural images. Each one has a uniqueness to her being that is God-given and God-ordained. The psychological truth of Bolen's archetypes will be true as well. The first three scriptural women tend to be independent in their orientation to the world. One will relate best to men, the second to women, and the third will be happiest by herself, but each is a whole person in her own being. The next three, however, find their identity in relationships. The archetypal wife, mother, and daughter personify women who are created to be intimately connected with others. And finally there is the one I have called the "catalyst," the one who activates personal transformation for them all. She transmits the energy of the divine to the others so that they may become whole. Her reality is part of every woman's psyche although she too may be the major force in some women's souls.

These scriptural archetypes all represent different facets of our Creator and are provided to us as heirs of the image of God. They give us energy, purpose, and direction as well as personal identity as women. We will feel the drive of several if not most of them in our lifetime, although one of them may seem to provide the major image of who we feel ourselves to be. For the most part the energies will be positive. They will empower and enable our work and our relationships. These are the God-given strengths of the archetype. When they are active in our lives, we reflect into the world the One in whose image we are formed.

Negative Energies

However, we can also misuse our gifts. We can utilize the archetypal energies in destructive rather than constructive ways. Jungians talk about the "shadow" side of our being, referring to those aspects of our psyche that are undeveloped or unknown or that we do not particularly like. Bolen talks about psychological difficulties that the Goddess archetypes may engender. I prefer to use the term "negative energies." Since God is Spirit, which is energy, and since God's grace is defined as life and light and love, which are energies, the archetypal powers are also energies and can be either positive or negative. "Negative" is not to be understood morally, however. Rather, think of the negative of a photograph as the reverse lighting of the final print. Or think of the positive and negative charges of a battery, both of which are needed to provide an electric charge.

The negative energies of the archetypes spring directly from their positive power. They are, however, distortions or inappropriate uses of their gifts. If we are unaware of the archetype within, we may be in danger of her becoming active in ways that are hurtful to us and to others. Or we may channel God's gifts toward our own personal power trips or ego enhancement rather than toward the creative purposes for which they were intended.

In Scripture there are women who represent the positive energies of the archetypes and others who exemplify the negative. The three independent women will each be paired, in order to more fully see both possibilities. The three relational types, however, will be presented as women who contain positive and negative energies within themselves. In fact, there is often a fine line between the two. It is often only the way in which a gift is used that we can call positive or negative. In looking at the differences in these women, we can better be on our guard against allowing the internal forces in our own being to propel us into avenues of action that we would rather not take.

Archetypes of women in Scripture, therefore, can provide us with the opportunity to combine psychological and spiritual truth in order to help find our lost sense of identity and worth. God has created women to be complete, whole human beings who can work for the healing of the created order.

Our task, then, is twofold. The first part is psychological: we are asked to identify for ourselves the positive archetypal energies that are our gifts. We are then to cultivate whatever others we may feel are necessary for our situation in life. It is probable that we will want to combine the strengths of one of the independent archetypes, one of the relational ones, and the power of catalyst in order to switch back and forth. We can then call on the appropriate ones at the appropriate times to help us on our journey toward whole, integrated selves.

The second part of our task is spiritual. Biblical archetypes enable us to accept our inheritance as daughters of God. They may also help acquaint us with some of the feminine attributes of the Deity and help us to worship a God who is fuller and more complete than the one we usually hear preached.

All of us, as we integrate the archetypes within and use their energies creatively in the world, can reflect back that part of the divine image that is woman. Until we accept that task, God's image will continue to be warped into the totally masculine shape that patriarchy has directed. We have been formed in the image of God. That is our spiritual inheritance and God's holy gift. By living out of this divine gift, we become psychologically and spiritually whole, fulfilling the intention of our Creator and representing to others the reality that we know is ours.

Let us, then, begin by looking at three independent women. You may find yourself reacting with an instantaneous recognition to one. She will be your archetypal reality, the aspect of the divine image that is your special gift. Take time as you read to fill out her attributes as you know her within yourself. Name the strengths you have already experienced and look for ones you may not have met yet. Also become acquainted with the potentials for danger, the possible negative energies that may erupt. Chances are that they may be familiar. Are the negative energies active in your life now? Perhaps one of the other archetypes would suit your present circumstances better. Think of the places and the times in your life when any of these archetypes have been helpful and ask how they can help you in the present. Become friends with all of these women and notice their power. The same strengths are offered to you and will be given to you any time you need them. Practice calling on some of the more familiar ones. You might hear their answer. These are your friends, part of the divine inheritance that has been given to you by your Creator. Your worth and value as a woman can be found in them. Once you know them and can enjoy their company as friends and neighbors, rejoice, call them over, and have a celebration.

PART
TWO

IMAGE

CHAPTER TWO

The Fathers' Daughter

A woman who represents the fathers' daughter is a woman of intelligence and inner strength. She is one who understands her own need for power and achieves it in a positive and socially productive way. She is naturally able to set goals, to strategize a plan for achieving them, and to implement her plan until she achieves what she set out to do. She is also able to change her plan if something else would work better or if something she has decided to do does not work as she thought it would. She is, in a word, adaptable as well as capable.

Think now of the successful women you know or that you have read about. Most of these women are good examples of this archetype. To look at them one sees neat, well-groomed individuals who know their own minds. They are aware of their goals and have a good idea of how to succeed at them. They get along well in the social order as it is now constructed.

The fathers' daughter is a planner and an achiever. She will make a success of herself in whatever field she happens to choose. She is also a survivor. It may, in fact, be this gift that underlies all the others. In a man's world, she knows how to either work the system to her advantage or to beat the system from within. She is not one to let circumstances dictate her life; rather, she is capable of arranging circumstances to suit her purposes. If and when the unexpected occurs or impending disaster seems to strike, she adapts quickly to the new situation and often turns it to her advantage. To paraphrase the cliche, she takes the lemons and makes a superb batch of lemonade. She will also serve it from an attractively arranged tray to the people who can best help her in her new situation.

Often, a woman of this archetype is a leader. The field makes no difference, whether she is in business or politics, law or medicine, teaching, social work, or volunteerism. She has innate abilities for decision making, adaptability, accountability, and responsible action that help her take the lead in most any organization.

Or she may choose to take the "back seat" in a corporate sense but in fact be the real power behind the throne. How many first ladies of this country have taken that course? The executive secretary may also be an example of this archetype. She organizes the office, arranges her boss's schedule, screens phone calls and visitors, and in general keeps the organization running smoothly so that business can be transacted neatly and efficiently. She is an invaluable asset to any office and worth her weight in gold, whether her boss is male or female.

Generally, the fathers' daughter tends to work best with men. She is, after all, a daughter of the fathers, of patriarchy, and not a victim nor an enemy of it. Quite the contrary, she will use the system to her advantage and will thrive in the competitive market economy that patriarchy enjoys. Men will see her as a colleague with whom they can relax and be themselves. They know they can count on her good sense and sound judgment to come to the heart of any dilemma and see possible solutions to it. She is, in fact, a superb problem solver. Whereas other women may lend a sympathetic ear to someone in trouble, this one will sort out the situation, come up with alternative solutions, and recommend strategic courses of action.

Recognizing the Archetype

Some women first recognize the energies of this archetype in themselves during their school years. I still remember the president of my high school senior class. She was extremely bright, but beyond IQ her intelligence was pragmatic and utilitarian. She could sort out complex issues and find ways, and people, to accomplish what was needed. She led meetings as one who was firmly in charge and yet was also open to suggestions. If someone had an idea that contradicted her own and could speak convincingly for it, she would be the first to embrace the change and offer ways to implement it. She worked well with both faculty and administration, for the fathers' daughter has no problem with authority. In fact, she is only uncomfortable when the chain of authority is weak or unclear. She is, in all ways, a systems person.

Other women come to a recognition of their archetypal strengths as a fathers' daughter when they enter the job market. If such a woman moves directly from school into work, she will probably look carefully at her options and at a given job's potential for advancement before making a commitment. She may well seek out the advice of a mentor, usually a male, who can pave the way for her into the organizational hierarchy. Once in, she will cultivate the contacts and friendships necessary for advancement and begin her road toward whatever she has defined for herself as success.

Her husband, if she is married, will look upon her as his best friend, which is most commonly the marital role she will take. She will be firm with her children and encourage them to cultivate their own abilities. She may be more partial to sons, but her daughters will be brought up to be like herself.

Women who stay at home for the childrearing years will be capable and efficient mothers and homemakers. It would be easy to stereotype them as super-moms, for they have the enviable ability to handle many things at once and do them all well. But this woman knows herself, and, unlike super-mom, she will not take on more than she can handle. Other mothers, lacking in the strengths that she innately owns, may be envious of her apparent "having it all together." But this will not bother her. She finds her friends with others like herself and among men.

Negative Energies of the Fathers' Daughter

As with all of the archetypes, there are two sides of the fathers' daughter. I have referred to them as the positive and negative energies. It is not that negative means "bad," but rather that some of her strengths may be misused if they are not adequately understood, or if she neglects to exercise her very real needs for personal power. For example, a mother who does not recognize that her way is not the only way may be very hard on a daughter whose archetypal reality is different. Or, being unaware of her power needs or having unwittingly allowed herself to be in a situation that she cannot control, she may use her strengths blindly and destructively. Few fathers' daughters would intentionally harm others to get what they want, but some, unaware of their own needs and impulses, may use negative techniques and strategies to gain their ends.

I once knew a woman who had reached late middle age without ever achieving what she wanted in life. She was frustrated, angry, and resentful. One could conceivably blame her for not going after her goals earlier in life, but she had been taught — as most women her age were — to be quiet, docile, and accepting. She had been a wonderfully supportive wife to her husband's career, but when he retired, she felt that her own life was meaningless. She joined a new church and immediately assumed leadership in the women's organization. Shortly, she was the president. This new role could have been perfectly suited to her needs; however, being unaware of these needs, she wielded her power like a knife. Many people were hurt by her techniques, for only her ideas could be put into effect. She became destructive to the organization, to the women around her, and to the church.

It is a scenario that unfortunately is echoed in many churches. The blame is not entirely hers. It is not that this woman was intentionally evil; it is merely that, being unaware of her unfulfilled need for power, she used her God-given strengths in devious and backhanded ways. She had fantastic leadership potential. The problem was that she utilized this potential for selfish purposes, for self-aggrandizement rather than for the church's good. As theologian Matthew Fox says, gifts that we are given are meant for creative purposes. If they are not used creatively, they will become destructive. The fathers' daughter who does not know her own strengths, or who denies or represses them, will probably become destructive toward others and herself.

Scripture gives us examples, archetypal images, of both sides of the fathers' daughter. In a number of biblical women we can see how God infuses us with the energies of this archetype and also how these energies can be used — and even must be used — for creative and constructive purposes.

Ruth and Naomi

One can think of many women in history who exemplify this kind of woman. In fact, most of the women who have made it into the history books of our patriarchal culture will be this kind of person. We think of female warriors such as Deborah and Joan of Arc, of a queen such as Elizabeth I, and even of modern heads of state such as Golda Meir and Margaret Thatcher. These women are true leaders, who take what is usually considered to be a man's role and who achieve great success. But most of us have trouble seeing ourselves leading troops into battle or governing a nation. And yet our archetypal energy as fathers' daughters may be equally strong.

Scripture has given us a more subtle picture of this archetype. It is the picture of one who works within the extremely patriarchal culture of the early Hebrew nation to ensure the survival of herself and those closest to her. It could even be said that in the story of Ruth and Naomi, God has reached beyond the limits of patriarchy to show women how to be strong. If there is not divine judgment against the male system in this story, there is at least divine instruction for women in using their God-given skills to adapt and survive within it.

The story of Ruth and Naomi is generally read as a tale of female friendship and fidelity. It is also seen as a lovely romance. It is actually very much like an archetypal fairy tale. Once upon a time there was a lovely young widow in the country of Moab who was left penniless and without a child. Rather than return as a burden to her family, she remained loyal to her dead husband's mother and stayed with her in her own grief and destitution. Because there was no husband or son to protect them, they were among the most vulnerable of all people. And so, together, they worked out a plan that would restore them to safety and well being.

The older woman knew of a distant relative, Boaz, who owned land in Bethlehem. To go there would be terribly difficult for two women traveling alone, but relying on God and on their own resources, they began the journey. We can only imagine the difficulties they faced along the road. The heat and dust, their hunger and thirst must have been terrible indeed. And how they must have longed for the days when Ruth's husband, Naomi's son, would have provided them with cool shelter, clean clothes, and the respect of their neighbors. But that was over now. They had to walk with their heads and eyes down, slowly, over the dusty roads.

Finally, they arrived at their destination and approached the large, prosperous farm of their cousin. But here they made a major decision. The two women refused to introduce themselves to Boaz as destitute relatives. They would not accept the victim's role. Instead, they used the skills we have identified as those of a fathers' daughter. Rather than begging and losing their self-respect, they drew up a plan that would get them what they needed and also restore them to their position in the social order. It was a plan that required time and patience, careful adherence to proper rules of behavior, and subtle seduction.

Day after day, the lovely Ruth entered Boaz's fields after his field hands had cut the grain, and she carefully picked up the leftovers as they lay on the ground. With these leftover stalks, she managed to keep herself and Naomi alive. She was also, of course, noticed by the wealthy owner of the field, who inquired as to who she might be.

Ruth never directly approached Boaz. That would have been unseemly. Rather, she gently lured him toward her. Finally, he offered her a scrap of bread, then a sip of wine, and the enchantment was done. She remained docile, hard-working, and loyal to her mother-in-law: all admirable qualities in any woman. But the final victory for the sweet young gleaner came when she entered Boaz's tent at night and revealed herself to him as a next-of-kin. Boaz, being an honest man, informed her that there was another who was a closer relative but that if this man would not accept her, he would.

The tension must have been unbearable for the women while they waited for the men to decide their fate, but in the end all was well. The other relative refused the offer, and Boaz was as good as his promise. So the loyal young widow was restored to her rightful place in society as the wife of a wealthy landowner. Her former mother-in-law was guaranteed a comfortable old age. And Ruth and Boaz, who were to become the great-grandparents of King David, lived happily ever after.

This is a charming story of female loyalty, and it is a sweet tale of romance. In fact, Goethe called this story the loveliest little idyll in the biblical tradition. But it is much more than this, too. It is also the story of two immensely practical women who used their brains, talents, and bodies to ensure the human rights that they had been denied through no fault of their own, other than that they had lost their male protectors. Rather than reading this story only for the lovely tale that it is, we can also applaud the clever strategy of Naomi and the clever seduction of Boaz by Ruth. These women are more than sweet, gentle victims who were rescued by their distant relative. They are strong, capable, intelligent, and realistic.

They were well aware that without husband or son, their position in society was little more than chattel. They also knew that to come to Boaz on bended knee might have gained them protection, but it would not have regained them their status. And so they strategized a very clever plan, patiently took the time necessary to put it into effect, and made sure that nature would take its course in the way that they intended it should. Reading their story as a frivolous romance robs these two strong women of the power they have to offer.

As women, we can learn much from their example. Not that we are to seduce wealthy men into marriage, but we can learn from Ruth and Naomi how to work within the system, oppressive as it might be, to gain the status that we want and deserve. As examples of women of patriarchy, as fathers' daughters, these two women show us the kind of tough thinking and intelligent, capable planning needed for survival in our world.

Our God has indeed gifted women with the skills we need to survive, and even to thrive. Some of these gifts are clearly exemplified by Ruth and Naomi, others will be discovered in other archetypes. The issue is that the gifts we have been identifying are parts of the divine energy imparted to these women by their Creator, as they are formed in God's image. These very creative skills in planning and strategizing, in using what was at hand, in adapting to what might have been a disastrous situation, and in carrying out the plan to achieve their goal are all aspects of the Divine made manifest in their actions.

Ruth's story is told and retold, her image immortalized in Jean-Francois Millet's "The Gleaners." Yet the value of her story goes deeper than we are accustomed to seeing. Her cleverness is a gift from God as God reaches out to her in her oppression. Throughout Scripture, the Holy One supports the weak. Our problem is that we often expect the intercession to come from outside of ourselves. Ruth shows us another way: to look within ourselves for the strengths that God has given us. Although patriarchy is not God's way, we are given the tools we need to work within its system and to succeed.

It must also be noted that part of the women's plan was the physical seduction of Boaz. Like Esther, Judith, and other heroines of the early Hebrew nation, Ruth used the beauty of her body to gain the power she needed. Modern women may wince at this strategy, but once again let us give credit to two very practical women.

Physical beauty has always been as asset in a man's world. Sexual attraction has always been at least one of women's greatest powers. I have been told by one man that we women have no idea of the power of our own sexuality. We may take it for granted, or we may be embarrassed and annoyed at men's stares and whistles, their innuendo and their sexual aggressiveness. But our sexual power is far greater than theirs, and we need to take this fact very seriously — and to use it very wisely.

Ruth and Naomi knew how to use Ruth's attractiveness to get what they wanted and needed. Seduction, even subtle, was the only power that they had in a rigidly patriarchal culture. It was a power given by God, and it was enough.

Negative Energies of the Archetype: Herodias

It is not difficult to see how even Ruth and Naomi skirt the negative side of the fathers' daughter. Their plan could be seen as manipulative scheming, were it not done for the women's survival. Ruth could be called a tease and a seductress if we were less inclined to view Boaz's attraction to her as just and part of God's will. But there are women in Scripture who do use these same coping skills in destructive ways. These stories, too, are given for our instruction and for our protection. The archetypal strengths of which we speak are powerful indeed, and to misuse them may be as disastrous to ourselves as it is to others.

The fathers' daughter: what is the reverse side of her considerable strengths? Perhaps the clearest example of her in Scripture is Herodias, the woman who is said to have caused the death of John the Baptist. We find her full story given in two of the Synoptic Gospels (Mark 6:14–29 and Matthew 14:1–12) and the results of her actions described in Luke 9:7–9.

Herodias was clearly a woman who wanted power. Her family history is very complex and incestuous, but Herodias, her first husband Philip, and her second husband Herod Antipas were all directly descended from Herod the Great, the one who ordered the slaughter of the innocents in Matthew 2:16. Herodias first married her half-uncle Philip, a relatively weak man whose political ambitions could not keep pace with her own.

When Philip's more successful half-brother, Herod Antipas, came to Rome to receive his investiture as the newly named tetrarch of Galilee and Peraea, Herodias seduced him and began her plot to become his wife. She persuaded Herod Antipas to divorce his own wife, and, taking their daughter Salome with her, she left Philip to join Herod in the new capital city of Tiberias on the shores of Lake Galilee. Now she had power, wealth, and status in the eyes of Rome and in the province that they ruled.

But one man was courageous and honest enough to cry "Foul." John the Baptist's call to repentance was not only a generalized call to the simple folk; his voice reached up to the very highest civil authorities, including the occupational ruler of Galilee. Again and again, John kept telling Herod Antipas that it was immoral to have married his half-brother's wife. More, he did it in a public and, to Herodias, in a humiliating way. Her husband, Scripture says, "feared John, knowing that he was a righteous and holy man, and he protected him. When he heard him, he was greatly perplexed; and yet he liked to listen to him" (Mark 6:20).

But Herodias had no such qualms. She schemed, she manipulated, she wove together a plot of revenge that is truly quite terrifying. As we are told in Matthew 14:1–12, Herod's step-daughter danced so pleasingly (and, we may infer, seductively) for him and his guests that he publicly granted her anything she wanted. Seizing the moment, as any strong fathers' daughter would do, Herodias told Salome to demand the head of the Baptist. And so it was done. Herodias stood unchallenged as the power behind the throne, the throne to which Jesus was eventually sent by Pilate.

Herodias epitomizes the potentially destructive power of a fathers' daughter. She was a schemer and a manipulator who used both men and women, including her own daughter, to get what she wanted. She also used sexuality. But it was not the kind of flirtation of Ruth, who sought legitimate protection and security. Herodias used the sexuality of her daughter, or at least the "pleasing" dance, to draw out of her husband the promise that would set her free from the Baptist's cry. The result of her destructive anger was the death of the one who was sent by God as messenger of the coming Messiah. Herodias can be seen as an example of this kind of woman at her worst, as one who had all the gifts of a Ruth or Naomi, but who misused them for destructive purposes. The Hebrew women made their plans to insure life; Herodias plotted a man's death.

There is, however, an interesting historical sidelight to Herodias. The historian Josephus tells us that her schemes continued, and that she, jealous of her brother Agrippa's even higher political position, persuaded Herod to demand the title for himself. Emperor Caligula had been forewarned by Agrippa of the pair's intent. Herod was banished to Gaul (France) in punishment, though Herodias was allowed to stay in Rome, out of Caligula's friendship with her father.

Here the story takes a strange twist: Herodias rejected the Emperor's offer of clemency and instead chose to accompany her husband into exile and disgrace. Why? Might there have been a transformation even of this woman? Josephus does not answer, nor can we do more than guess. But perhaps the Baptist's plea was finally heard and repentance came even to this pair. So, perhaps, did the mercy that Jesus preached. We can never know, but it seems that even the destructive, jealous rage of a Herodias may not be her final identity and reality.

A potential danger for a fathers' daughter may very well be the misuse of her strengths, but even this horrifying example of what seems to be true evil may have an ambiguous ending. The negative energies may not be as ultimately destructive as we may first assume. They are, after all, merely a perversion of what is a gift of God. Perhaps Herodias needed to experience her own worst before she could be transformed to something better. Hopefully, she put her strengths to more creative use and worked alongside her husband as they governed the province of Gaul. It could be suggested that if she had been allowed the power of the men in her family in the first place, she might not have misused her gifts as she did.

The denial of opportunity may in fact be a real and present danger for women of this type. Energy will be expended, either positively or negatively. Fathers' daughters will need to find ample ways to expend theirs wisely.

Integration for Today's Fathers' Daughter

What, then, do the fathers' daughters of the Bible have to say to modern women? How do we incorporate their positive, God-given strengths in a healthy and creative way? And how do we protect ourselves from these same strengths when they are used unknowingly or unwisely? A personal example may help.

For the first ten years of my married life I stayed at home and raised my children. I had been told in subtle and not so subtle ways that this was my role in life. Somewhere I had even gotten the impression that this was God's intent for me as a woman — that it was God's intent for all women. My college degree and teaching certification were "just-in-case" insurance, protecting me against the terrible possibility of being on my own.

After ten years of this, however, I timidly began to venture out of the house. I began volunteering in schools and church. Surely this was within the bounds of acceptable behavior. But my involvement grew, and, under the mentoring of a strong man, I began to take leadership positions in these organizations. Then I took on a part-time teaching job and accepted a staff position at the church. My responsibilities multiplied.

My archetype was hooked. My husband and I divorced when it became painfully clear that I could not go back to the old way and he could not accept the new. Then I became an administrator. I was good at it, too. I made plans with formal goals, strategies, and objectives, and achieved real success in meeting these goals.

But after a while, my daughters' pain erupted in a way that even I could not ignore, and I began to assess what I had done. I saw how I had capitalized on my husband's weaknesses during those years at home in order to feel my own unexercised strengths. I saw how I had hurt people at work in order to get my plans across. In fact, someone once told me that I was known at work as "the iron maiden." I saw how I had ignored my daughters' confusion when I shifted archetypes so radically, and how I had put my needs so far above theirs. Although the things I had accomplished were generally constructive and creative, the means by which I had achieved them were not always so.

This was not a happy time for me, but it was instructive. I am now familiar with the fathers' daughter within me, and I have learned to treat her with respect. She is strong and demands that I utilize her powers. If I do not do so constructively, she becomes very nasty. And so we try, most of the time, to be friends.

Many of us do have a need for power, and all of us need skills to survive. These needs may be met in various ways, but they must first be acknowledged in order for them to be dealt with fairly. Part of the difficulty we have in meeting our need for power is that we have been taught to be reactive rather than proactive. That is, most of us have learned to respond to others, rather than to take the initiative ourselves.

We have also been taught to be self-effacing and to let others take any credit. The fathers' daughter who accepts the role of the power behind the throne may find satisfaction in this. Others, however, will not. These women will need to learn to be assertive in making their ideas known and in finding the people and resources to carry them out. They will need to assume responsibility for themselves, take risks, and learn to be accountable for their failures as well as their successes. The fathers' daughter who is well integrated within herself will also work with others rather than use them. She will help build up others' confidence and potential because, in the long run, their strength only makes her job easier.

Because fathers' daughters generally work best with men, they need to be aware of using their sexuality inappropriately. Ruth used her body in a very different way than Herodias used the body of her daughter, and for a very different purpose. I do not believe that it is God's intent that women should have to entice a male protector to take care of us. But given the world in which Ruth lived, she used what she had in order to survive. The Ruths of today will joke, more or less seriously, about marrying a man for his money. Some will use sexual seduction to lure him on. In this world, it is a real temptation. Besides, for a fathers' daughter, the chase is a real challenge; it is just plain fun!

Perhaps other aspects of the archetype might be better employed instead. Women can succeed in today's world by the creative use of their God-given gifts: practical intelligence, sound planning, adaptability, accountability, and personal (not just sexual) attractiveness. Moreover, these gifts, or energies, can be strengthened even in women for whom this archetype is not a major aspect of their being.

It may help to remember that our Creator has given all of us coping skills and that the kind of skills we have been discussing are all part of the divine Source of life that we call God. Fathers' daughters are created in God's image with power born of God. They can be real leaders in today's world. Or they can be survivors in situations where other women may fail. But their first task, as for all women, is internal: to recognize the gift — to whatever degree they have it — and to purposefully direct it into positive avenues of action. To ignore it is either to impoverish ourselves or to let it surface on its own. If we do the latter, however, we will not be in charge of where it may lead.

The issue, then, is responsibility: responsibility to the archetypal energy that is God's gift within. Naomi and Ruth show us how to use this energy to survive and even to thrive in a man's world. Herodias warns us what may happen if we let our own ego gain control. Use — or misuse? The choice is ours.

Questions for Reflection

You might, given these thoughts, ask yourself to reflect upon the fathers' daughter within yourself. Who is she? How long has she been there? Do you use her gifts? Do you feel her energy? How do you exercise her power?

1. *Can you remember a time when you adapted well to a difficult situation? What happened?*

2. *When do you take responsibility for yourself? In what situations do you abdicate that responsibility?*

3. *What do you do when you feel powerless?*

4. *What are your present goals in terms of self-fulfillment? Do you have a plan?*

5. *What concrete steps do you need to take to meet those goals?*

6. *Who will support you in those steps?*

7. *When will you implement your plan specifically?*

CHAPTER THREE

The Sister

injustice and calling for reform. Needless to say, if she is called by the One in whose image she was formed to follow this path, her way will not be easy. New history books of women's achievements, however, are filled with examples of those who have courageously accepted such a call.

My Sister Joan

In thinking more personally about this archetype, I seem to assume that she is a mature woman. Perhaps this reflects my older sister's influence. Although she is also very much a wife and mother, Joan has the keen intelligence, honesty, straightforwardness, concern for justice, and independence that this archetype embodies. She is a natural leader and has held several sensitive political positions.

Beyond that, I see her as a person who is very much aware of herself as a woman. She was one of the first to help form a consciousness-raising group in her area. She still remains friends with many of these same women today, some fifteen years later. She has been a real friend to me: one who not only listens but helps to clarify and seek solutions. Like the archetype, she is not a game player but sees to the heart of a situation or relationship and demands honesty in discussing it. She does not spend time sending long letters or even calling frequently, but she is a woman on whom I know I can depend. It seems fitting that all four of her children are female, and not at all surprising that she has tried to bring them all up to be strong, professional women with lives of their own. Joan is a woman's woman, a sister in the most archetypal sense of the word.

One other facet of this archetype is the sister's connection to the natural order. Since we still assume "Mother Nature" and "Mother Earth" to be the domain of the female, most, if not all, women find this connection to be true. Long ago, of course, the Creator was worshiped and revered as a woman because of her miraculous creative work of conception, gestation, and birth. The archetypal sister, the woman's woman, is one who has not lost contact with this sense of divine connection with the earth that all people once had. She is one who will find great healing energy in solitary walks by the ocean or in back-packing the Appalachian

Trail or in taking camping vacations into the vastness of the western states.

A teacher friend of mine, clearly an example of this archetype, spends her vacations climbing mountains. Sometimes she takes a friend — often a female, though not always — and sometimes she goes alone. She has climbed in the Rockies and in the Alps and in the Himalayas. Wherever she goes, she finds eating and sleeping on the land and the pleasure of reaching a summit extraordinarily powerful. As she says, both the challenge and the intimate embrace of nature's wildness refill her soul and rekindle her with enthusiasm. She returns from each trek exuberant. And, she also returns from each climb more satisfied with her strengths as a woman.

Negative Energies of the Sister

The archetypal sister needs to know herself well. Although her gifts are many, her very strength may make her dangerous to herself and to others. For example, her passion for justice may make her merciless toward either an offender or a passive victim. She has little patience with either. The sister is not interested in excuses for irresponsible behavior, whether it results in damage to others or to herself. She can also be cold and cutting in her directness. She may be adept at putting someone in his or her place if they try playing games with her or if they are less than candid in her presence. The sister insists on truth no matter who it might offend.

A greater danger of this archetype is, however, to herself. Because she refuses involvement in the stereotypical sexual relationships between men and women and because she may concentrate all of her energies on her career, she may find herself lonely and isolated. Moreover, she may become so frustrated at the patriarchal assumptions and expectations all around her that she simply cuts herself off from everyone. The sister needs to find an environment where her particular strengths are appreciated.

The sister may also run into trouble because of her goal directedness. Whereas the fathers' daughter may be tempted to use others to get what she wants, the sister is apt to simply push people out of the way. Her impatience with other folks' weakness may cause profound pain. Moreover, her insistence on doing things on her own and doing them as quickly as possible may be very difficult for those who prefer a more relaxed, collegial style. If she is working with others, she will need to be more aware of their different abilities and ideas than she would normally be. On the other hand, if they will accept her considerable skills, things may be accomplished more simply and rapidly than otherwise.

Judith

The sister, like all archetypes, is merely one aspect of the divine image. Women reflect many facets of the brilliance of the Creator; this archetype shines with her own particular brightness. Her many strengths and skills, of course, are given to her by God for a reason: for particular and creative use in this world. Often she channels her considerable energies into issues of justice. Other times, she is seen at the forefront of a new concept or movement.

Several women in the Hebrew Scripture exemplify this archetypal nature: Miriam, the sister of Moses, who sang and danced in victory at the Israelites' crossing of the Red Sea (Exod. 15:20–21); the five daughters of Zelophehad, who went to Moses to demand their rights of inheritance (Num. 36:1–12); Jael the Kenite, who drove a tent peg through the head of the enemy Sisera after Deborah's army had defeated him so badly (Judg. 4:17–22). In the New Testament, the clearest example is Lydia, the dye merchant and head of household who first hosted Paul's beloved church in Philippi (Acts 16:13–15, 40). But it is in the extracanonical writings known to Protestants as the Apocrypha that we find the woman most representative of the sister archetype.

Judith is considered one of the great heroines of the Hebrew people, and for that reason she is given a book of her own name. We first meet Judith in the first verses of chapter 8; she is portrayed as a docile, pious young Hebrew woman. Immediately we are given the impression that there might be more to her than meets the eye.

We are told that she is mistress of a large estate left to her by her late husband. She did not hire a foreman, or any male, to oversee her holdings for her. Instead, we are told that it was her maid who had charge of all her property (8:10). It would seem that not only did Judith believe that women were capable of handling their own financial affairs, but she also had some very interesting ideas when it came to the role played by a so-called servant. These were clearly two very strong and independent women who felt no need to find men to help them survive.

Their land and their people were, however, in jeopardy. King Nebuchadnezzar of Assyria had sent in an army, and his generals were demanding surrender. The magistrate and chief elders of the city, facing a siege in which the people of the town were probably going to die of thirst and hunger, were about to capitulate to the enemy's demands without a fight. When Judith learned of their intentions, she summoned them to her home.

This was a woman who did not wait to be asked her opinion; she assumed that she had a right to be heard. Judith went beyond merely giving her opinion, as any archetypal sister will when she senses the need for immediate action. Holding firmly to her faith in a God who did not want Judah destroyed, she mercilessly chastised them for their weakness and lack of trust.

"Listen to me, rulers of the people of Bethulia! What you have said to the people today is not right," she asserts in verse 11.

"Who are you to put God to the test today, and to set yourselves up in the place of God in human affairs?" she demands of the faithless men in verse 12.

"You will never learn anything!" she charges in verse 14, explaining to the men the divine intentions of the God who had promised them the land.

Incredibly, the leaders listen quietly and accept her insults without denial. They give her a weak excuse for their actions like small boys caught doing something wrong by their mothers. One can almost see Judith's angry defiance as she lectures the men on their cowardice and their lack of faith. And one can picture the men, shamefaced and hanging their heads, as they acknowledge that she is right. They try to escape by asking her to pray for them (8:31), but Judith refuses to sit back any longer and watch others destroy what God obviously wants to retain. Instead, she tells them that she will take matters into her own hands: "I may go out with my maid; and within the days after which you have promised to surrender the town to our enemies, the Lord will deliver Israel by my hand" (8:33). Even more incredibly, she does not ask them for advice, affirmation, nor permission to do what she has planned. Instead, she tells them, "Do not try to find out what I am doing; for I will not tell you until I have finished what I am about to do" (8:34).

Judith, true to her archetypal nature, saw the situation clearly and took matters very firmly into her own hands to bring the justice that she saw as warranted. The fathers' daughter would never act as Judith did. Like Deborah, the fathers' daughter would have sought out generals and troops to fight back. Only a sister would insult the leaders of her town and do the deed herself without even informing them of her plan.

Judith's actions from then on were those of a strong and courageous woman. She first washed herself and removed her widow's clothing in an act of consecration of her new role to God. She dressed herself as attractively as possible and, with her maid, entered the enemy's camp. Since women are rarely seen as a threat, especially to soldiers, and especially if they are attractive, they had no trouble being allowed inside. Once among the Assyrians, Judith easily led them to believe that she was seeking sanctuary. Naturally, the general in charge, Holophernes, was impressed by her courage and her beauty and invited her to stay. Judith, however, received permission to leave each night to go into the desert and pray to her God, supposedly so that the sins of her people might be revealed to her.

In this regard, Judith is very much the archetypal sister. Many women like her will find that they pray best in natural surroundings. They often prefer the sounds of wind and waves to the majestic choirs of cathedrals. They hear God better among birds and animals than in the midst of a well-dressed congregation. Judith, however, was not only following her natural tendencies. She was also setting up a situation in which she would be free to leave without question when she had accomplished her task.

Four days later, Holophernes had determined to get Judith into his bed, and so he invited her to a sumptuous dinner served with a great deal of wine. Judith, drinking only from the supplies she brought with her, remained very much in charge of her faculties. The general, however, drank himself into a stupor. Seizing the moment, the docile little widow of Bethulia cut off his head with two swipes of his own sword. She then calmly wrapped it in some netting and handed it out to her waiting maid, who stuffed it into her food bag. The two women then calmly walked out of the camp as they had done the three days before, and returned to their town.

Seeing Holophernes's severed head displayed from the battlements, the Assyrians fled in total disarray, the town was saved, and Judith's name was entered into the annals of history. We are told that she never married again although she had many suitors, that she lived to be 105, and that she gave freedom to her faithful friend and maid (16:22–23). Judith was truly a woman of courage, independence, intelligence, and amazing inner strength. Her fight was not only for her own survival, but as the text makes clear it was on behalf of the people of God and the survival of the Hebrew faith.

This kind of woman may be feared, but she is also respected. If pushed, she may indeed take matters, or the sword, into her own hands, but her main consideration is faithfulness, and faithfulness involves justice. The archetypal sister will not tolerate cowardice. She will set a goal based on what she knows is right and do what then needs to be done.

The Negative Energies of the Archetype

As with Ruth, the fathers' daughter, the positive and negative energies of this archetype are not far apart. Judith was a woman's woman, an independent fighter for justice, a goal-oriented person who went straight after what she wanted, a woman with a keen and quick intelligence. Although cutting off an enemy's head with his own sword may have been considered just in the late Bronze Age, we may allow ourselves some pause at what this says about the archetype and her methods of achieving success.

The sister will do whatever is necessary to achieve her goal. If this goal is blocked by another, then that person will be moved aside, one way or another. If she has determined that she is right in a given situation, there may be no room for negotiation. She can become rigid and unyielding regardless of the discomfort she brings to those around her. Although people admire her considerable skills, they may tend to keep some distance from her for their own protection. Thus she may become isolated because of the thoughtlessness caused by her own disciplined absorption in her task.

The archetypal sister will also need to be very careful about her own righteous anger. Because her sense of right and wrong is so keen and because she is quick to jump to the defense of the victim and bring justice to the oppressor, she may allow her usually well-disciplined emotions to get the better of her. Lashing out in anger is not always beneficial, no matter how just the cause may be. The sister is particularly vulnerable to inappropriate reaction against anyone who threatens either her or her beliefs, or attempts to abuse her in any way. Anger or rage may well be channeled into constructive avenues of action, but they can also be devastating if allowed to simmer in silence, pour out indiscriminately, or leak out in sarcasm and put-downs.

These dangers of the archetypal sister stem directly from her substantial strengths. They are not evil or sinful attributes within her being. They do, however, represent dangers of which she needs to be aware. This is part of her responsibility to herself and to the One in whose image she is formed. Her independence will direct her into doing things in her own way in her own time. There are few checks or balances on her actions unless she invites them. Deliberately cultivating a more collegial style of work may be an important way of overcoming, or at least protecting oneself against, some of these negative energies of the archetype.

Delilah

One woman in Scripture seems to have fallen prey to several of the more negative aspects of this archetype although her strengths are also obvious. Delilah was the woman with whom the mighty Samson fell in love (Judges 16). The leaders of her people, the Philistines, came to her to ask her to rid them of their powerful enemy. Like Judith, she took matters from there into her own very capable hands.

The story is, in a way, a wonderful tale of a woman's cleverness and a man's stupidity. Samson was, however, more than a muscleman who went around doing strange things like killing men with jawbones and setting foxes' tails on fire. He was also a judge of

Israel and had successfully led his people for twenty years before Delilah destroyed him. He could not have been a totally ignorant man, but he was completely undone by this smart young Philistine woman.

Delilah's task, her goal, was to discover the source of Samson's strength, which, in fact, came from God. His mother had consecrated his life to Yahweh in gratitude for his miraculous conception. As a visible sign of this consecration, Samson was not to cut his hair. When Delilah began questioning him, he was careful not to reveal the truth. He told her that if he were tied up with seven fresh bowstrings, he could not escape. She tied him up with seven fresh bowstrings and called in her compatriots. Samson easily broke free. A second time she begged him for the truth. This time Samson told her that he could be overcome with bonds of new, unused rope. Again, she tied him up and called the Philistines, and again Samson broke free.

One would think that Samson would have gotten the picture by now, but since it makes a better story, the saga continues. Delilah, true to her archetypal nature, was no quitter. She must have wondered how long she could get away with what she was doing, but she had her goal and was determined to succeed. One more time she asked the question, and one more time Samson lied, but it was clear that he was wearing down. This time he did allude to his hair; he told her that his weakness was in having it woven and pinned down. One more time, she tried and found it to be untrue.

Finally, after days and weeks of persistence, Delilah learned the truth. This woman would simply not give up! She had his head shaved, and Samson was undone. Instead of being killed, however, his eyes were gouged out, and he was put in prison. Death would have been kinder, but Delilah was not interested in being kind. Her people took back their land and planned a great victory celebration, during which they brought Samson in to entertain them while they made fun of his degradation.

But by now time had passed, and Samson's hair had grown back in. With one last cry to Yahweh, he ripped the pillars of the hall from their foundations and killed everyone inside — including himself and, presumably, Delilah.

Some have said that Delilah, being a heroine to her people in the same way that Judith was to hers, should be honored rather than reviled. Certainly her skills and independent strength were no less. But like it or not, the Bible was written from the perspective of the earliest people of our faith. We can now look back and see victimization and oppression where they saw simple justice, but we cannot put twentieth century thinking into the minds of late–Bronze Age humanity. We must, then, look at Delilah from the perspective we are given.

Although we can admire her courage, her intelligence, her perseverance, and her clear focus, we must also say that her methods were less than positive. She was merciless, ruthless to the man she had pretended to love. She used her body and the immense force of her sexuality to entrap the man so that she could destroy him. Delilah may be appreciated by some as an example of many of the strengths of this archetype. However, it is also clear that in her case, as in so many others, the positive and negative energies of her powers were dangerously close together. In the eyes of most, Delilah unquestionably crossed the line.

Integration for Today's Sister

How can we put together the positive strengths of this archetype and incorporate the power of the negative without falling victim to it? Perhaps it is best to begin by reminding ourselves that the sister is a woman created in the image of God. From that point of positive affirmation, we can dare to look at the perversions of her God-given strengths when they are allowed to go awry.

Righteous anger provides energy to seek justice and to right wrongs. Even pent-up rage can be directed into correcting the oppression that has been done. Anger, psychologists tell us, is neutral. It is neither right nor wrong. What we do with it is what requires ethical consideration. We cannot ignore the plain fact that any of us is capable of murder, given the right circumstances.

Many women's first reaction to feminist awareness is an almost uncontrollable rage. Anger springs up from depths we were not even aware of. Women, in general, harbor years, even centuries, of unspent rage. It is at the root of most of our illnesses, particularly depression. With awareness of our own willing participation in years of oppression, this rage bubbles up and often spills over. It can be enormously destructive, to ourselves as well as to people around us. It can also provide energy for reform.

Becoming actively involved as an agent for change can tap into this energy as little else can. Discovering the secret of patriarchy's power and then using it to destroy, as Delilah was able to do, killed her as well as Samson. Using powerful energies to change what is unjust is an altogether different use of the archetype's strengths.

The sister will need to remain ever vigilant about what is in charge: her rage or her mind. Women are indeed capable of murder. Some think that destruction, at least in terms of the patriarchal system, is warranted. But we would do well to heed Delilah's warning before going too far lest we bring the walls of the building down on ourselves as well. Prayerful acceptance of our strengths may provide us with alternative ways of righting the injustices in the social order if we accept the responsibility that is ours to do so.

Friendship

Another important aspect of the sister archetype is female friendship. Judith and her maid clearly had a relationship that was unique, at least for their time. They were more than employer-employee; the maid was much more than a servant. Instead, they worked together, protected one another, and trusted one another implicitly. Scripture tells us that they remained together for the rest of their lives, and that Judith gave the other woman her freedom.

That is a beautiful statement. How many of us have lifelong female friends? And how many of us can give another woman her freedom? Judith accepted a very precious gift when she decided to treat her maid as an equal rather than as a servant. Would that we all could find another woman with whom we can share our hopes, our dreams, and our work. Women can sometimes understand one another and work together in a way that few male-female partnerships are able to achieve, no matter how deep the love between them.

When women gather together to share journeys and skills, new networks of deep empowerment emerge. Whether it is a coffee-klatsch of preschool mothers or a feminist consciousness-raising group or the rapidly growing networks of businesswomen, women who are aware of this archetype within themselves will naturally seek out other women. Again, real damage is done when women become so compulsive in what they are doing that their relationships suffer. Friendships with other women are important too.

Integration for Today's Woman

Integration for the archetypal sister also means consciously taking time to feel connected to the earth. Judith knew what she had to do only by going into the wilderness to pray. Others like her may need to schedule regular walks in the woods or on the beach. It will keep her well grounded and focused on the task she has been called to do. She may also make the environment itself her task, becoming involved in critical environmental projects. Her anger and sadness at the rape of the earth may provide her the positive energy necessary to bring about change. Justice for creation would be a cause in which an integrated representative of the sister would excel.

Along the same lines, the sister is one who will need to take good care of her body, even as Judith carefully prepared and consecrated hers to God before setting out for the Assyrian camp. Women have been told for so long that our bodies are dirty, ugly, and shameful that some of us still have trouble ridding ourselves of the old tapes. It might help to read about some of the early women's rituals that anthropology is beginning to discuss.

It used to be, for example, that a woman's menstrual cycle was a holy, sacred time. All of the women of a given village or tribe were often on the same lunar cycle, and at their time of the month they would all meet together in the women's tent to celebrate their creative power. Their blood would flow freely onto the ground or into a stream as they washed, and they would feel their intimate connection to the Great Goddess whom they worshiped.

Many modern women have lost touch with the powerful complexity of their bodies. Others are helping them to reestablish contact within themselves. It is part of the reconnection to natural forces and to our Mother Earth. In these days, the connection is not only pleasant and fulfilling for us as women, it is vital to our ecological survival.

The sister may have a difficult time in the institutional church. She may yearn for more open, natural, creative forms of worship. She may readily accept God and Goddess as simply two faces of the same divine reality and thus wince in pain at the sexist language and symbols still so pervasive in the churches. Still, her strengths are gifts of that divine reality no matter what others may name it. She has been called to be the person she is and to do the work of the New Way in any capacity she can. God needs sisters to bring the Spirit's unsettling breeze into the musty old churches of patriarchy's domain, even as God has called sisters to bring reformation to the social order.

The sister's vision is imperative today. It is not by chance that women of this stripe are becoming as prevalent as they are. It is by divine intent. Our responsibility is to look within ourselves and find the reality of the sister there, and then to practice her skills.

Some women have long recognized the sister within. For others, however, her appearance may be a traumatic experience, especially if they are in middle age when it occurs. Many of these women find that they have lived most of their lives as fathers' daughters, as wives, or as mothers. They have no positive images for or experiences with the sister archetype. They have not felt that her kind of independence was a viable option for their lives.

With the women's movement, the flood of books and articles being written, and the host of positive role models, however, they have begun to touch an energy within themselves that they had not previously known was there. Often it presents itself first as rage toward all that has prevented them from getting to know this part of their reality before. But in time and with the help of others like themselves, most of these women have rechanneled their energy into ways that make a difference in this world. In their new work, regardless of its challenges, they have felt an immense relief at coming home to themselves.

Questions for Reflection

1. *Think of a strong, independent woman you know. How are you like her? How are you different?*

2. *When what is important to you or your faith is being threatened, do you do something about it? If so, what do you do?*

3. *Do you have a woman friend who is a sister to you as you are to her? Describe your relationship.*

4. *Are you in touch with your rage? If so, has your rage ever been destructive? What happened?*

5. *How can you use the energy of women's rage in positive and constructive ways?*

CHAPTER FOUR

The Wise One

T hus far we have met two of the three independent women, women who tend to be very active in the world. The fathers' daughters and the sisters of our world, and in ourselves, have distinct personal characteristics that focus them outward into society and bring them competence and success.

The wise woman represents a third way of dealing independently with the world. Also a person of great strength, capability, and personal power, she may not be as obvious as the other two. Her power lies less in her achievements than in her internal being, less in what she does than in who she is. Personal power is a matter of being. Wise women are centered, quiet women who appear to harbor within a deep, intuitive knowledge, even a secret knowledge, a special kind of wisdom. These women never appear to be ruffled or anxious, harried or stressed. Instead, they always seem to be at peace, even in the turmoil of work, home, and family.

There is a wonderful Hebrew word, *shalom*, which, among other things, means "equilibrium in the midst of chaos." It stands for balance, integrity, and wholeness — in a word, peace. This is a peaceful woman. Her home or office will have a tranquil atmosphere that even a casual visitor can appreciate. People will feel comfortable in her presence and may allow themselves to lower defenses often firmly in place to the rest of the world.

Unlike her two independent sisters, her focus is not on a future goal, an achievement, or some success. Unlike them, her considerable energies tend to reflect inward rather than radiate outward into the world. She lives deeply for the moment, savoring and relishing each and every minute of each and every day. She may be very involved in the world, either within the established order or working against it. She may be single, or she may be a wife and mother. But she will not be defined by any one role. She is very much her own person and will live and enjoy her own life as her inner sense of being demands and directs.

In most discussions of archetypes, the wise one is imaged as old. But women who identify with this archetype feel her presence from a very early age. We have all met some young girls who seem wise beyond their years. They seem to harbor an uncanny understanding or wisdom that is somehow ageless. Throughout their school years, their peers quietly seek them out to ask questions, to seek guidance, or simply to feel the reassurance of their quiet, nonjudgmental spirit. As they mature, they may well become teachers, counselors, or spiritual guides.

The wise woman often radiates peace, and her company offers a space and a presence as comforting as it is strengthening. She is a superb listener. She may not offer advice in terms of problem solving as the first two archetypes might; she is more likely to help someone see what is behind a given situation. She is more in tune with causes than with effects. As a counselor, she is less likely to practice behavior modification and is more comfortable helping folks interpret their dreams.

A wise woman enjoys meditation and prayer. She responds to yoga and quiet contemplation. Her truth comes from within, and she reflects on what others tell her in this more contemplative way of knowing. Being aware of her own being, she is not a woman who will try to define others. Rather, she will help them to look within and to identify the person that they are.

Negative Energies of the Wise Woman

The wise woman can use her gifts unwisely, however. Morton Kelsey and other Jungians warn us about the dangers of the unconscious. There is a force of evil as well as a force of good. Today there are many ways of tapping into the deep unknown: Ouija boards, tarot cards, spiritualism, channeling, automatic writing, and simple ESP, to name but a few. Astrologers, palm readers, and eastern gurus all claim to be able to discern the word of truth; some, to foretell the future. Who is to say what is dangerous and what is not? Parapsychology and metaphysics are as close as Shirley Maclaine or *Nightmare on Elm Street*.

How do we know when someone is speaking out of their God-given gifts and when someone else is merely manipulating people's natural interest in the unknown in order to make a buck? How do we discern? Perhaps the most important questions we might ask would be something like this:

1. Is this message affirming of life?
2. Does this message illuminate my understanding of God?
3. Is this message compatible with the Gospels' teaching on love?

Women who feel themselves strongly in tune with this archetype need to be aware of the negative forces that would encroach upon their gifts. These gifts are not strengths to be taken lightly. They may be extremely creative and helpful; they can also be inordinately destructive. The gifts are from God, but how we use them is up to us. Whether the energy of this archetype is utilized positively or negatively may depend to a large extent upon our own grounding in faith. The wise one will need to define for herself the Deity whom she serves.

She may well comprehend a God who is, in fact, much more vast and inclusive than the God to whom the rest of us generally pay lip service. Nearly thirty years ago, J. B. Phillips wrote a little book entitled *Your God Is Too Small*. The wise ones will readily understand Phillips' point. They know intuitively a God who reaches and expands beyond all limitations, boundaries, definitions, and images. Their very inclusiveness is a balm to the marginalized who come to see them. Moreover, their unconditional acceptance of all that is life affirming, light directing, and loving helps others to appreciate the limitless vastness of the loving force known as God.

Wise women may face two relational difficulties, both stemming from their strengths. The first is what Jungians call a lack of persona. Most of us tend to be different in work or in public than we are at home. We put on a mask, so to speak, to appear to the world as we want to be seen. We may, for example, put on a strong, capable mask in the office even when we are feeling weak and vulnerable. Or, we may put on a genial, sociable mask at a party even when we feel miserable. But the wise one usually does not wear a mask. She is who she is. For this reason, she may seem more vulnerable and less capable than she really is.

Her other relational difficulty may be isolation, but for a very different reason than that of the sister. This is a highly introverted, introspective woman. She is very happy to be by herself and needs no one to validate her being or challenge her to be all that she can be. She is, instead, a woman who finds deep fulfillment in solitary activity, who can profoundly enjoy being alone without being lonely. But without making an effort at sociability at least some of the time, she may find herself alone more than is healthy for her.

Usually people will seek her out, and she will not run into this problem. But when she moves into a new neighborhood or a new job, the responsibility to meet others may first be hers. She may find this very tiring and difficult. Soon, however, she can settle into her new routine, others will begin to notice her aura of serenity, and they will come to bask in its calming effect.

Huldah

One of the most important women in Scripture is a woman like this. Not surprisingly, we rarely ever hear about her although her intelligence, wisdom, and insight preserved for us the great Hebrew lawbook of Deuteronomy. Her story is documented in 2 Kings 22:14–20 and 2 Chronicles 34:22–28.

Huldah was a prophet who lived during the time of King Josiah. It was a fateful time for Judah, following the fall of the northern kingdom of Israel. King Josiah was trying desperately to recapture the faith of his people by reinstituting some of the Mosaic laws and restoring the temple. He was convinced that the northern kingdom had been overcome because of its disobedience to Yahweh and that Judah might be saved if it would repent and become faithful once again.

During the renovation of the temple, workers discovered an ancient scroll. When the high priest realized that it was a book of the ancient law and read it to the king, Josiah tore his clothes in repentance and despair. He then sent his high priest, his adjutant general, his personal attendant, and other trusted men to the home of Huldah in order to "inquire of the Lord" (2 Kings 22:13).

Although the high priest was able to read the document, later known as the Deuteronomic Code, the king still felt it necessary to seek Huldah's advice. The cognitive intelligence that recognized both the words and the worth of the written message was still not able to discern its deeper significance. The men knew what the scroll said but not what it meant. For this, they needed the wise one. Frequently this will be so. Others may be intellectually adept, even brilliant, in academic circles, but it will take the wisdom of a woman like this one to discern the meaning behind the message.

Huldah's message to King Josiah was harsh. She told him that divine retribution was indeed coming to Judah because they had not been faithful. She foretold the coming defeat of the southern kingdom and the dispersal of the Hebrew people. But Huldah was also the interpreter of God's mercy. Because Josiah had done all he could to turn his people back to Yahweh, the destruction would not occur during his lifetime.

Women of wisdom are not cruel or unnecessarily judgmental. Although they will be honest in their appraisal of a situation, they will not use their gifts to punish. They will leave justice up to God.

Josiah heard the words of the Lord as Huldah fearlessly delivered them and proceeded to institute some of the greatest programs of reform seen in Old Testament times. He brought all of the people, the inhabitants of Judah and Jerusalem, the priests, the Levites, and all the elders together at the temple and read to them the words of the lost book. They then covenanted with one another to reinstitute the commandments, laws, and statutes that Yahweh had delivered so long before. They destroyed all of the idols and false gods that had worked their way into the worship of the people.

Josiah and his people then celebrated the Passover according to the book of the law:

> No passover like it had been kept in Israel since the days of the prophet Samuel; none of the kings of Israel had kept such a passover as was kept by Josiah, by the priests and the Levites, by all Judah and Israel who were present, and by the inhabitants of Jerusalem. In the eighteenth year of the reign of Josiah this Passover was kept (2 Chron. 35:18–19).

All of this occurred because of the gifts of Huldah the prophet, to whom the king sent his top advisors in search of wisdom.

Huldah does, indeed, personify the soul of a woman of wisdom. Rulers sought her out for advice; her message was tough; but her word was accepted as the word of Yahweh. Four times we read in these short passages in 2 Kings and 2 Chronicles, "Thus says the Lord." Huldah was not an oracle, uttering words of her own devising out of a trance. Rather, she was a channel, one could even say a medium, for the Word of God. Her communications stemmed from an attitude of life, light, and love, the trinitarian attributes of the Divine.

Women like her may or may not be able to make predictions based on an intuitive knowledge of where following a given path may lead. But the wise woman will probably, like Huldah, be one whom others seek out for guidance and direction. Unlike the fathers' daughter, she will not actively involve herself in what her words may initiate. Rather, she will remain quiet, centered, and peaceful like the eye in the midst of a storm. What is important to recognize and to remember is that she may be the eye at the center of each of us if we take the time or if we have the courage to seek her counsel.

Jezebel

In Scripture people who are called out and set aside to hear God's voice are called prophets. They are recognized by their neighbors as those who have the gift of receiving and transmitting the word of God. It is a position of extraordinary power. There are, however, in Scripture, as in today's world, negative energies even in this archetype. There are false prophets as well as true ones. Through them, we can see the dangerous side of the intuition that is the wise one's greatest gift, and we can begin to understand how she may respond to the evil energies of reality rather than to the positive energies of grace.

There are — it is interesting to note — very few examples of false female prophets in Scripture. One would almost expect, for example, that witchcraft or sorcery would be a relative common female heresy, given the vast numbers of women later burned and tortured as witches in the name of Christianity. Scripture, however, is not as brutal.

Perhaps the most infamous of them all is Jezebel, whose story is found in 1 and 2 Kings. Jezebel is introduced to us as the wife of Ahab, king of Israel (1 Kings 16:31). She was a native daughter of Phoenicia and thus worshipped Baal and Asherah. As queen, her strong native faith overpowered her husband's apparently weak faith in Yahweh. Together, they erected statues and temples to her deities and fed some 850 prophets of Baal and Asherah at their table (1 Kings 18:19). Jezebel's evil is described and her deeds denounced in many ways but always in reference to her religion. She was a woman profoundly identified with her faith.

Her major opponent was the prophet Elijah, and even he ran away from her. Like the wise woman archetype, she was deeply attuned to her gods and lived her life according to their leading. Jezebel was determined that the God of the Hebrews would not supplant the gods her people worshipped. She therefore tried to have all of Yahweh's prophets destroyed. Elijah escaped.

Jezebel survived her husband by a decade but died as one of the Hebrew prophets foretold. She was pushed out of a tower onto the streets below where stray dogs ate her body, leaving only her skull, her feet, and the palms of her hands (2 Kings 9:30–35).

Jezebel's story is less about a specific woman of history than it is about a person who worshiped and caused the Hebrew people to worship other gods. Her faith must have been overpowering to have controlled her life and actions the way it did. If she had been a prophet of Yahweh, imagine how valuable she might have been! Jezebel, then, represents a woman who has deep intuitive knowledge of the divine and who lives in terms of her beliefs. But rather than being centered in a Deity of life, light, and love, she was deeply embedded in the forces of death, darkness, and destruction.

If Elijah radiated positive energy, as he must have in order to revive the widow of Zarephath's son (1 Kings 17:17–24), so Jezebel radiated the negative. This is not to say that Jezebel, her gods, or goddesses were necessarily evil, but that her intuitive awareness was badly off the mark. Rather than having shalom at her center, she must have had something akin to the raging dogs who finally consumed her body at the end.

The wise woman will need to be aware of where her allegiance lies. The problem most of us have is that our focus is external. We do not trust our own intuition to tell us who we are. In fact, we have been told so often that our intuition is fantasy, we have come to believe it ourselves. We also, if we are being very honest, prefer to worship idols. We like to be comfortable. We want to be secure. We are not happy rocking the boat. We really do not want to ask too many questions. Many of us actually resent anything that demands extra time or energy. We cannot face the conflict and confusion of change, even when that change involves personal growth. But prophecy demands no less.

Integration for Today's Wise Woman

God has spoken to and through women from the very beginning of the faith. Time and time again women have been called to speak, to serve, to direct, and to lead God's people into ways of peace. Today, women are being called by the hundreds, even the thousands, into ordained and lay ministry. God's call of women to direct and active service is being affirmed by congregations and denominations around the world. Is this any different from what God has been doing for four thousand years?

Women who turn a deaf ear to God's call and churches that refuse to affirm God's actions are denying much of their own tradition. They find proof-texts that refer to the dark side of women or to the cultural, patriarchal bias that unfortunately has found its way into our Scriptures. But they cannot refute what history has told us. As Jung once said, Scripture is the Word of God; it is not the words of God. Focusing on the literal, specific words is little more than another idolatry.

When those words are used to deny the wise one her rightful

place as an inheritor of the divine image, when she falls prey to false patriarchal teaching and sexist biblical interpretation, she may indeed fall victim to the negative forces of reality. In this, she can hardly be blamed. But it need not happen. Perhaps more than any other of the archetypes, the wise one needs to hear the affirmation of her reality as a child of God created in God's holy image. Her own intuition will tell her that it is so, but if she is constantly told the old patriarchal lies and put-downs, her sense of being will be as confused and distorted as Jezebel's, and her gifts may become destructive or may be lost entirely.

Huldah was able not only to read the specific words of the Deuteronomic Code, she knew what the words meant. Reading the entire document in the light of her knowledge of Hebrew history and tradition, she could name the sin that had led her people to the brink of disaster. She could state what had to be done, and she could predict the consequences of both Israel's sin and Josiah's attempt to reform. This, perhaps, is wisdom: the ability to recognize what *is*, based on what *has been*, and from that to anticipate what *will be*. This means that the wise woman always needs to have an open mind.

It also means that a wise woman must be courageous. She must be willing to share her gifts with those who seek her out and not be afraid of their response. Some wise women will be ready to help people discern Scripture in new and perhaps different ways. Today's Huldah may or may not be ordained, but she is very much alive. She may be a counselor or a teacher or one of the feminist biblical scholars with their hermeneutics of suspicion and deconstruction. She may also be seen among the women theologians who are pointing out all of the positive images of the feminine in the being of God. Her archetypal image has been evident in the quiet mystics of our faith and in the gentle Quakers who formed the Underground Railroad for liberating black slaves.

The wise woman of today will allow her intuitive powers to instruct her carefully. Like Huldah, she will utilize her God-given gifts to read between the lines and to look beneath the surface. She will be sensitive to the distortions and patriarchal preferences that men have been taught and preached for so long. Something inside of her, her center, will tell her that what she has heard is not true. This may be profoundly disturbing and unsettling. For her, truth is more than a matter of intellect. She must feel it in her very being and receive affirmation in her bodily awareness before she can accept it as fact. She, therefore, will often find herself in the position of seeker, as she allows the truth about her Creator and herself to slowly sort itself out. Many women who enter seminaries or attend workshops or conferences find themselves in this position. The answers they seek are not vocational in terms of a job but vocational in terms of a calling to personal authenticity. These women are seeking deeper answers than the ones they have been given.

Workshops and conferences are, in fact, a valuable place for the wise one to go. She may shy away from the crowds and stay on the periphery of the activity. But she will, if she is conscientious, find profound encouragement in the sharing of life journeys or spiritual pilgrimages. If she can overcome her natural introspection enough to tell her story, she will have a wealth of intuitive experience and knowledge to share. She will also receive affirmation of her own gifts as people naturally turn to her for guidance.

Women who are comfortable and well integrated within this archetype know the importance of listening with a third ear. When they are with another person, they listen: first, to the words that are said; second, to their own minds and intuition; and, third, to a voice from within that provides objective and comprehensive insight into the whole process. Some call this voice the Spirit; some call it Wisdom; some call it the voice of Christ or even of God. Some say that the name does not matter and that it is all the same thing coming from the same divine source. The wise one is one who is innately attuned to that inner voice.

All women can develop it, as all women can develop the skills of the fathers' daughter or the sister or any other of the archetypes. But it is the wise one whose sensitivity or receptivity is most acute. She has much to tell the rest of us if she can stay centered, overcome her natural reticence and preference for solitude, and share what her soul knows. Moreover, when she is serene and balanced within herself, we can see without being told the reflection of at least one facet of the radiance we know as God.

A Time for Reflection

To better acquaint yourself with the degree to which this archetype is within you, you might practice a short meditation. Read each paragraph, then put the book down, and let your mind and body relax.

First, take three deep breaths, then release them slowly. Let any tension flow out from your head . . . your forehead . . . your jaw . . . your neck and shoulders. . . . Let your breathing become shallow as your relaxation increases. Imagine your body dissolving as you release all the tension in your stomach . . . your hips . . . your thighs . . . your knees . . . and finally your feet. Let any negative thoughts or energies surface, and then watch them evaporate into thin air and disappear.

When you are totally relaxed, image the center of your being. Go there and stay for a while. Listen to your heart beating. Feel your blood rushing through your body. Let your soul expand and relax with your lungs.

Now let your visual eye move more deeply still. What is there, in your very center? Stay there and enjoy your self for a while. . . . When you return, you will feel refreshed and renewed. You will also know how very close to you is your God. Let the peace you feel stay with you. The world around you needs what you have to give.

Questions for Reflection

1. How are you aware of the wise woman within?

2. What are you doing to cultivate inward serenity?

3. Do you remember a time when you had specific spiritual insight? Did you act upon it? How?

4. What idols tempt you to false worship?

PART
THREE

IMAGE

CHAPTER FIVE

The Wife

The first three archetypes are all independent women. That is not to say that they do not have significant relationships, for they do and will, but their primary identity is not derived from relationship in the way that the next three will be. The woman we speak of now, the archetypal wife, presupposes a life partner. Her personal identity is fulfilled within the bonds of that relationship; her attitudes and actions are determined by her sense of responsibility toward it. The archetypal wife is a woman who commits herself utterly; once she has found her mate, her decision is for life.

This type of devotion has obvious strengths but clear dangers as well, especially in terms of potential victimization and abuse. Some women will live with any behavior from their mates in order to remain within the relationship, but this is not a necessary aspect of the archetype. The wife is, rather, a strong woman who commits her life to making a strong marriage.

Her relational skills are innately her own, but she will also go out of her way to learn more. She will observe other relationships and take note of their strengths and their weaknesses and then borrow from the positive traits in order to strengthen her own. She will read the latest materials on good communication skills, on fighting fairly, on how to realistically share household tasks. She feels it her responsibility to cultivate the best marriage possible and will work hard to make it so.

The archetypal wife today has many more options than she did in the past in terms of her own life. She also has a much wider range of relationships with both men and women. Like most women, she will undoubtedly have to work outside the home, but her self-fulfillment will not come through success on the job, as it will for the first two independent archetypes. This woman will work because it is necessary for the well-being of her marriage. Her satisfaction will come from carrying her share of the financial burden of living in today's world.

She knows that forcing her partner to be the sole breadwinner may be damaging to her mate's health. It is also patently unfair — and she knows it — to expect her mate to endure the hassles of the marketplace and to carry full responsibility for their financial security. She has read the statistics on males' early death rates and the prevalence of heart attacks, and she will take steps to see that her status of wife does not suddenly change to that of widow.

Because she respects herself for who she is, the wife has no problem envisioning and working toward an equal partnership with her mate. This mutuality and equality will manifest itself in many ways: in terms of domestic chores, financial responsibility, and social interaction, along with others. Beyond the obvious, though, it will also be evident in the bedroom.

This is a woman who will accept her own role in sexuality; she will be as actively involved as her partner. She will initiate sex as often as her mate and will readily swap roles during sex play. She will be open to discussing her sexual likes and dislikes as much as she will be eager to learn what pleases her partner. Sexuality, for the archetypal wife, will be immensely important and vital. There will be a sacredness to her lovemaking that will make it profoundly spiritual. The very act of sex will be to her a sacramental union in which she finds total and complete fulfillment. When she is making love, the wife will feel complete and whole, as if her entire being had been touched by God, which may, in fact, be true.

Beyond Stereotypes

Part of the problem in discussing the archetypal wife is that we tend first to think in terms of stereotypes, and the stereotypical wife is very different from the one I have just described. The little woman who sacrifices her name and herself to her husband's every whim, and who cannot know herself apart from his reaction to her, is a negative and destructive picture of what should be an archetype of considerable power. If the wife is created in the image of God, she will not be the stereotype that most people imagine. God does not harbor a side of divine reality that enjoys humiliation or abuse. Nor does God call anyone to be oppressed under the domination of another. There are many possible dangers to the woman who identifies herself primarily as wife, but the dangers come from social sickness and not from archetypal energies as they are given by our Creator.

Modern society — that is, Western white society of the past 150 years or so — has defined the role of wife in a generally negative way — and then has pronounced it good. It has taken hold of the very positive strength of her commitment and turned it into an attitude that says that women must stay with their men "no matter what." Even when she is emotionally or physically battered, the wife has characteristically been told to go home and mend her ways so that he will not be forced to reprimand her again. Too often, the archetypal wife has accepted this perverted view of herself and has either done as she was told or has left the abusive situation feeling guilty that the relationship has ended. This is, indeed, a perversion. The archetype is a strong woman, not a weak one. Commitment for her takes the form of active engagement, not passive resignation or victimization.

Even a woman in a generally healthy marriage can fall prey to the dangers of her own strengths. She may tend to neglect relationships other than her primary one. She may feel less than comfortable with women who are not half of a pair. Because of her emotional investment in the relationship, she may become jealous of her partner's career commitment or friendships with other women and men. But these are distortions; they are not part of the archetype itself. They are, rather, a misuse or misinterpretation of the archetype. They may also occur when a woman is unclear about the strengths she has inherited and when she allows her mate to tell her who she is.

The archetypal wife is not simply a mirror reflection of her partner. She is a woman who innately has within and who intentionally cultivates skills of intimacy, commitment, and love. These are difficult skills to acquire and difficult ones to exercise. They demand constant attention and constant work, but the rewards are also generous. A woman who lives her life out of these archetypal energies can look back in old age and feel good about the love she has shared. She will feel that her role as wife has far outweighed in value any money, success, or even fame that she has earned in a career. For her, that one primary relationship defines her life and is her life. As with other archetypes, God created her to be a particular kind of woman. Her fulfillment of that task is enough.

The Creation Accounts

"In God's image" is both a gift and a promise. The divine image is a gift imparted to each and every human being. It means that we are each inheritors of divine grace, and that each of us is a tiny reflection of one of the facets of God. The promise is that we will be given God's help to mature into a being in whom that reflection becomes visible. By living out our archetypal nature as it has been given to us, we can co-create with God a fragment of divinity on earth.

Often, if not always, there is a huge disparity between the gift and the result. The promise is often left at least partially unfulfilled — not on God's part but on our own. We refuse, for whatever reason, to accept our responsibility to become the people we were created to be. The writers of the Hebrew Scriptures grappled with the problems of human suffering and sin, trying to account for why we neglect the gift as it is given. Many of the great epic stories of the Pentateuch are symbolic ways of describing their theological understanding.

No text in Scripture has received as much scrutiny as the first three chapters of the book of Genesis. The various interpretations of the creation narratives have caused unbelievable discord and contention. They are the basis for patriarchy's claim to male supremacy and the long-held prejudice that calls women evil. They have been misinterpreted as equating sexuality with original sin and thus denigrating one of the Creator's most beautiful and sacred gifts. Most unfortunately and unfairly, Eve is still believed by many to be the temptress who lured poor Adam into sin.

There is profound truth in the biblical accounts of the Creation, but the truth is more poetic and symbolic than it is scientific. To many of us, the former is the greater. Science, as wonderful as it is, still cannot define God — although physicists are sometimes more inspiring than theologians in describing the powerful, creative energy forces of light, life, and love.

The creation narratives do impart truth, but that truth is not as obvious as it would appear. What they do attempt to do, in a symbolic way, is to point to the mystery of God the Creator and to the miracle of life. They point to the sovereignty of God over all creation and, in particular, to God's relationship with humankind. They tell a story of a "fall," a division between the Creator and the creation, and in that story attempt to find meaning for suffering, pain, anger, guilt, and sin. Beyond all of this, they examine the profound and divine relationship between feminine and masculine, between male and female. They also define the archetypal wife as God created her to be and then sadly describe the perversion of her gifts.

The Priestly Account

In order to carefully pull out this definition, we need to separate the two accounts of creation. The first we find in Genesis 1:1–2:4a. It is known as the Priestly or P account. The second account begins at 2:4b and goes to 3:24. It is known as the Jahwist or J document. Authors P and J wrote at very different times and for very different purposes.

Chronologically, J came first. It contains the story of the Garden of Eden and the saga of Adam and Eve. It is unknown exactly how old this story is, but it was written down centuries before the P document and was undoubtedly centuries old before being written down. The P account, the first verses of Genesis, was not written until after the Babylonian exile in the sixth century B.C.E. It is a theological statement and not a story. It is carefully constructed with repeated phrases, even parallel refrains:

> God said, "'Let there be a dome . . . ." (Gen. 1:6).
> "Let the waters . . ." (v. 9).
> "Let there be lights . . ." (v. 11).
> "Let the waters . . ." (v. 20).
> "Let the earth . . ." (v. 24).
> And God saw that it was good. . . . And there was evening and there was morning, the first [second, third, fourth, fifth, sixth] day (vs. 4–5, 8, 12–13, 18–19, 21, 23, 31).
> Then God said, "Let *us make* humankind. . . ." (v. 26).

Here we have a difference in the refrain that signals that something unique is about to happen. Here we are introduced to a whole new level of creation. Genesis 1:27 reads:

> So God created humankind in his own image,
> in the image of God he created them;
> male and female he created them. . . .
> and indeed, it was very good (v. 31).

According to biblical scholars, the English word "humankind" was originally the Hebrew word *ha-adam*, a derivative of the word *adamah*, meaning "earth." Literally, the new being is an "earth creature," a living thing with no discernable gender. Next, we find that the earth creature is plural, a unity of both genders, female and male. God formed humankind in God's own image, simultaneously feminine and masculine, female and male. God's image is not male. It is more than that. God's image contains both masculine and feminine reality, what is called "androgyny." But God's reality is also far, far greater than that. God both includes and transcends gender.

Humankind, both male and female, is given dominion over the rest of creation: a creation, but the way, that is designed by God to be vegetarian. There was to be no aggression or killing, even for food. This "dominion" seems to be a far more benevolent caring and tending than we have cared to understand (see 1:29–30).

This highly polished poetic and theological narrative of the

creation of human and fe/male unity was given the primary position in Scripture by those who compiled the canon. Its truth is clear:
God created woman and man simultaneously in God's own image.
Behind this statement lies mutuality, complementarity, affiliation,
connection, and equality. The more theologically sophisticated
Hebrews of the postexilic period crafted an exquisite narrative that
described their understanding of the perfect and complete beauty
of God's creation as it was intended. It is a peaceable kingdom,
indeed.

It also gives us our primary picture of God's intention for
humankind and for the relationship between man and woman. The
earth creatures who are formed in this section of the narrative are
not married, but they are in the kind of complementary and complete relationship that marriage seeks to emulate.

If God's image is, among other things, a perfect blending of
male and female reality, then the wife must look carefully at that
image to help determine her role. It is unfair to say that because
God created male and female together, all humans are incomplete
without a mate of the opposite sex. In fact, the story says more
clearly that androgyny is primarily an intrapersonal reality rather
than an interpersonal one.

Some women are called to help recreate within the social
order the wholeness of ha-adam. This is the archetype of wife. In
this part of the narrative, we catch a climpse of what her call and
her original image might have been. Today's wife is given the holy
task of reestablishing at least a likeness of this original unity. To do
this, she must be the equal of he; if either is dominant, wholeness
cannot be restored.

The Jahwist Account: Ishshah or Eve?

As beautiful as this first account might be, we must look at the
earlier account as well. This is the story of Eden, of a "man" made
from clay and a woman made from "man's" rib. This is the story —
since the P narrative does not do it — that is used to "prove" male
supremacy. But does it?

Once again, the created being called "man" in English is not originally masculine but an earth creature, *ha-adam*, created from earth, *adamah*, and given by God the breath of life. The earth creature then was moved into the garden prepared by God (Gen. 2:15) and was given the mandate against eating the fruit from the tree of the knowledge of good and evil. Only then does God decide to separate *ha-adam* so that relationship and sexual intimacy may be enjoyed.

God causes a deep sleep to fall upon *ha-adam*, who awakens as *ish* and *ishshah*, two beings formed from a single source in the image of God. *Ishshah*, woman, and *ish*, man, are created as equal partners in the garden. They are naked and without shame (2:25). Of course. Is one shamed by one's own body? Not in the eyes of God. The couple feel and celebrate the unity that was theirs as *ha-adam*. There is no sense of difference; the two are still as one. Thus the first part of the narrative ends. *Ishshah* and *ish* are free to romp and play in their garden home, in unity with one another and in God-given relationship to the entire created order. It is as it was meant to be. This is what God intended, and it is still what God wants: love, mutuality, and unity between man and woman; responsibility and obedience to God.

This, then, is the archetypal reality to which the wife feels herself called. As *ishshah*, she is to live in the world with her partner as separate aspects of the same substance. Essentially, they are one although physically they are two. Differences between the sexes are no more significant than the differences between a hand and a foot. They are simply different. One is no better or worse than the other; one is no more important than the other. They are neither embarrassed by their physical differences, nor do they feel that one is more beautiful.

The archetypal wife is, at a deep level of her being, profoundly aware of this androgynous symbol of wholeness. This is the power she feels when she is making love. In those moments, she comes as close as is humanly possible to rejoining *ish* and *ishshah* into *ha-adam* once again. It is, indeed, a holy and sacred act. But the image defines the rest of her calling as well, in terms of cultivating her half of the totality as he is to cultivate his. They are equally responsible to the gift and to the promise.

The Fall

But the tale goes on. Genesis 3:1–24 tells the story of the Fall. The serpent, the catalyst for the action of the story, is one of the most ancient and most powerful symbols for woman. It is not, however, described as the devil or Satan or even as evil. Nor is it an image for sexuality. It is merely the tempter. Jung suggests that it represents the invitation to wisdom. *Ishshah* believes the promise that no harm will come to her if she eats the fruit. Why should she not? She has not yet learned about deceit and guile. She tastes the fruit, and it is good. She offers it as a gift to her mate, her other half, and he docilely accepts it. In this tale, she is the active one, he is passive. She acts, he responds. But the responsibility belongs to both. They act as one.

Genesis 3:7–24 describes the consequences of the act. For the first time, *ish* and *ishshah* see themselves to be separate and different from one another. Against the intention of the Creator, the one becomes two. As they become aware of their separation, they feel shame and so cover their genitals as those bodily parts that most obviously mark their difference. When God comes to stroll in the garden, they hide. Guilt and fear, along with shame, are born.

When asked to explain, *ish* projects blame onto *ishshah*; *ishshah* projects blame onto the serpent. Unity disintegrates: (1) between *ishshah* and *ish*, (2) between the *ha-adam* and God, (3) between the earth creature and the rest of creation, and (4) between woman and her most sacred symbol. No longer is she a part of the Great Round of life, death, and re-birth. Now, there is only death. These are the consequences of disobedience. Instead of pleasurable stewardship of God's creation, man now experiences labor, hardship, and toil. Instead of joyful intimacy with man, woman now experiences oppression, uncertainty, and frustration. Instead of being at one with herself, her feminine symbol, woman's identity loses its meaning and its power. After their banishment, then, *ish* and *ishshah* are given the separate names of Adam and Eve. No longer are they one being, one soul. Unity has been destroyed.

The stereotype of wife comes almost directly from this richly symbolic tale. One of the real tragedies in Scripture is that the original Hebrew words *ishshah* and *ish* are not used, so that the difference between the original creation and the consequences of the "Fall" is not as clear as it might be. We tend to look at Eve as undergoing a radical change, one which can never be turned around. If we keep the separate words in mind, however, we can return to both the original hope and the promise.

Eve, the name of fallen woman, is the result of both the man and the woman's sin. The original pair should really be discussed in the singular rather than the plural, as the names *ish* and *ishshah* suggest. But at the end, Eve is definitely her own person, separated from Adam. When God predicts the consequences of this separation, the words speak to Everywoman in terms of her capacity to give birth, her symbolic knowledge of herself, and her connectedness to creation.

But they also speak directly to the archetypal wife. The harmony and unity of God's design for her have been shattered, which means that men will seek domination over her and that she will experience oppression under male rule. Those are the predictions of God, and they have more than come true. They have even become the stereotypical image of the archetypal wife, but they merely describe the negative aspects of her situation. They do not define who she is or who she is meant to be.

When she plays out the victim role instead of the one God originally gave her, the archetypal wife is reenacting the energies of the Fall. This is not to blame the victim for her own oppression; rather, it may help women to see that they do not have to take the abuse they are being given and provide them with the energy they need to break free. Also, when she cuts herself off from single women and any man other than her mate, she is living out God's sad predictions. When she becomes jealous and possessive, she is turning her back on her original call. And when the wife realizes that she is losing herself in trying to be what the social order tells her, she is suffering the consequences of society's sickness and not being faithful to her Creator's intent.

All of these negative forces at work in the archetypal wife are to be feared, but they do not have to define her life. The woman who is faithful to the original blessing of her creation can accept both the hope and the promise as they were symbolically given so long ago, and so become the strong person she was intended to be.

Integration for Today's Wife

What does this mean for today? All we need to do is to read a book on marital counseling to see the results of guilt, fear, projection, and blame. We need only to look at sociology, anthropology, politics, economics, medicine, law, and institutional religion to see feminine oppression. We only need to turn on the radio or television, see a movie, or read a magazine, book, or newspaper to observe male "supremacy." The consequences of the Fall are legion, and they are everywhere. They are surely the basis for the stereotypical wife. But do they define the archetypal one?

Who is the archetypal wife? Is it *ishshah*, created with her mate in the image of God? Or is it Eve, the condemned woman after the fall? The way we answer this question leads us far beyond theological hairsplitting. If the archetypal wife is Eve, then males and females are destined to spend eternity in opposition to one another, out of relationship with God and the rest of the created order. But if the archetypal wife is *ishshah*, there may yet be hope. In fact, if the primary reality of the sexes is not *ha-adam*, who became *ish* and *ishshah*, then we have to deny or ignore God's intention in creation in order to continue living as we do. Perhaps this denial is our greatest sin, even our "original sin."

Today, perhaps more than any other time in history, women and men are taking a new look at what it means to be husband and wife. Modern women are no longer willing to accept Eve's sentence and be submissive, quiet, docile, and self-sacrificing. They are looking toward relationships of love based upon mutual respect, appreciation, and responsibility. They are aware that their lack of involvement in the economic and political realities of their lives is not only detrimental to themselves as persons, but it is also literally killing their husbands. It is not selfishness that is leading us back to *ishshah*'s worthiness but concern and compassion. If helping to shoulder the burden of financial responsibility with our partners will keep them alive, that alone is worth it. To refuse to do so may, in fact, be the greater sin. To allow ourselves to receive second-class pay and second-class stature is hurting others as much as it is hurting ourselves. And it is certainly hurting our families.

The archetypal wife in today's society, then, has an enormous challenge. If she is a woman who is already married, she will do well to reassess her role. There will be strong societal pressure for her to accept the stereotype of Eve rather than the original archetype of *ishshah*. She will need to resist this pressure and look instead to the strong and positive relational skills that she has been given. She will know the enormous satisfaction and challenge of committing oneself totally to someone else. Although no relationship is without pain and difficulties, she will have the positive energy of her archetype behind her to work with her mate toward solutions to their problems.

Her most important challenge will, however, be herself. It will be easy for her to forget her own needs and ambitions in deference to her partner's. But unless these needs and ambitions are faced, she will no longer *be* a partner; she will simply be an image of her mate. The archetypal wife has the responsibility of being as strong in herself as she wishes the relationship to be. That means that she may need to build up other more independent aspects of her personality. Whether she recognizes the fathers' daughter, the sister, or the wise one within her being, she would do well to activate this archetype's strengths as well as her own. In this way she can more readily carry her weight in the relationship and help to create the kind of mutuality that God intends.

Wives Without Husbands

But what about single, divorced, or widowed women? How do they fare if this archetype is demanding satisfaction and they are not in a significant relationship? For many women, this is a serious and painful problem. Women today may be afraid to commit themselves to marriage because they fear that the stereotype may hook the archetype within and destroy them. Or they may wait in order to concentrate on their career, knowing instinctively that as wives, they would shift a major portion of their energy away from the job. Or, they may deeply yearn for the kind of mutual relationship that they know is God's design but cannot find a man willing to share it with them.

There are no easy answers for these women. Perhaps they might shift some of the focus of their strengths from husband to their career or to their friends. Commitment, personal growth, and relational skills are all necessary in various aspects of life. It is obviously not the same, but it might help release some of the energy.

Lesbian women who are of this archetypal nature may well find fulfillment in their relationships. But they will need to be aware of stereotypes as well. The lesbian who identifies herself with the archetypal wife may find herself dealing with the same dangers as her heterosexual sister. The positive strengths will be the same, but so will all the temptations of the negative.

Divorced women who identify with the wife will find the humiliation and pain almost too much to bear, often assuming all of the responsibility for the break. Some will search as soon as possible for another man. Others will spend a lifetime staying emotionally married to the man who has left. The archetypal wife probably ought to spend several years getting back on her emotional and financial feet before making another permanent commitment. But she will need to do some honest assessment of her role in the previous marriage, the reason she married the man she did, and the reasons for the break. Only when she is satisfied that she either did all she reasonably could or was all that she could reasonably be expected to be, will she have the positive strengths to begin again. She may need some help in defining what is reasonable because she will probably tend to be too harsh on herself. The time taken for this task will be well worth it.

Statistically, widows who experienced a good marriage the first time are more apt to marry again. Health and opportunity permitting, this may be so, but it is not always the case. Others might fall into the danger of thinking that their man was the only one for them and so spend the rest of their lives in grief. Perhaps, though, even if she cannot find another suitable mate, she can grow to accept her new status and use the same strengths and skills she used in her marriage in other areas of life. If the tens of thousands of older widows in our society are financially and physically able, there is no reason why their lives must emotionally end with their spouse. Life will be radically altered, and the loss may never fully heal, but they can learn, in time, to devote their considerable abilities outward toward the needs of the social order in service to others even less fortunate than themselves.

The archetypal wife is a force of considerable power. She can influence her mate, her children, and her society. Returning to the archetype of *ishshah* may be an avenue by which she can reclaim some of her great gifts. The road from the fallen Eve to the woman created by God may not be as long as she thinks.

One wife who was painfully moving from a stereotypical understanding of her role to a more archetypal one had the following dream. First, she was with a group of seven very old women who were gathered around a round stone table (an altar?), studying religious texts. She sensed them as Wisdom and felt that they had something very important to tell her — a profound and ancient secret, a profound and ancient truth.

But before they could speak, the woman found herself in a church, sweeping the floor of the nave. She was anxious because there was not much time to complete her task. Suddenly, she looked up and saw a man sweeping the chancel. She was furious! In fact, she was so angry that she woke herself up. He had no right to be interfering with her task! What was more, he had no right to be closer to the altar than she.

When she told me this dream, I simply asked: "Why wouldn't you let him help you?"

Her anger dissolved in tears, and she began to understand. The man and the woman needed to work together. The wise old women had given this second dream as the answer to the first: Only by working together would they approach the altar of God. Only in mutuality will the archetypal wife find peace. She cannot create a marriage alone, and neither can her partner. But if she will accept her share of responsibility and insist that her mate work by her side, they may be able to sweep out the old stereotypical concepts of wife and return to the one provided originally by God.

Questions for Reflection

1. *How do you accept the idea that you are the one primarily responsible for the relationship with your mate?*

2. *Have you ever felt like a victim? What happened, and what did you do about the situation?*

3. *How do you take care of your own needs?*

4. *What are your greatest strengths in your primary relationship?*

CHAPTER SIX

The Mother

T he second of the archetypes defined by relationship is mother, one of the most universal archetypes of all. There are vast differences in her image as her physical features change from culture to culture and from race to race, but the reality behind the images is timeless.

When we look back to the earliest manifestations of civilization's celebration of maternity, we are overwhelmed by the number of myths, legends, religious cults, and mystical rites that surround the Mother Goddess. She was ubiquitous. Virtually every culture around the world worshiped some form of her being. She was responsible for the creation of the earth; she often was portrayed as being the earth. She gave birth to all of life; and, she could not be separated from all of life. She was chaos, the void from which all existence was birthed.

She celebrated the lunar cycle within her own body and was regent over the seasons of the year. Spring was her maidenhood; summer her fertile glory. Fall and harvest celebrated the fullness of her wisdom, and winter declared the cold reality of death. Yet even death was not final; it was merely a part of the Great Round of life. Death only prepared the fallow fields for replanting in the spring. Decay enriched the barren soil in preparation for new life. Death was only another face of the creative Mother of all existence.

The ancient myths of the Mother Goddess often connect her with a daughter. In some, she is both mother and daughter. Her various names include Inanna in Sumer, Demeter in Greece, and Ceres in Rome. There are significant variations in these myths depending on their age, but the major story line remains the same. The Great Mother and her daughter (who may also be either a younger self or an inner child) are one. They are carefree and happy, loving one another and embracing all of life. Creation rejoices in their joy, and nature overflows with the fecundity of the Goddess's creative juices. Crops and fields grow ripe and full, and water flows freely through the warm, moist earth. There is harmony in creation, and her children are fulfilled.

But this beauty cannot be sustained. She decides to go to the underworld (in the earlier stories) or her daughter is abducted there (in the later myths). The earliest story of the descent provides the archetypal shape of a woman's coming to maturity, and we shall look at that more closely when we discuss the image of the daughter. At this time, however, our focus must be on the later myth of a mother's love — and of her pain — when her girl-child is forcibly taken from her. It is the reaction not only of a woman who has cruelly lost a child but of a woman who has lost a piece of herself.

The story thus begins with a lyric description of the beautiful relationship between mother and daughter. One cannot help but smile with the images of Demeter's love for her young child. The two of them romp and play together among the flowers. They whisper secrets and laugh out loud at the antics of the animals. The mother offers herself unconditionally for the pleasure of the child, and feels complete in the giving. In the myth, there is no other family; the focus is on the two alone. This simplicity allows every archetype of mother love to become visible. Her devotion is totally on the child. Her delight is in the generosity of her care. Her greatest joy is in watching and helping the child to grow.

Giving birth is one of the most miraculous moments of a woman's life. Whether the child is a son or a daughter, the wonder of it all far outweighs the agony of labor. The archetypal mother will not feel whole until and unless she has had this experience. She will play mother to her dolls or her younger siblings at an early age. She may baby-sit the neighborhood children through her teenage years. All along, she will be preparing for the day when she can have a child of her own.

As soon as she feels that the time is right, she will find her life's fulfillment. Her joy at the first missed period will only increase as the days go by. Even early nausea and fatigue will be embraced as part of the wonder. As her body changes, her breasts fill, and her belly swells, she will sometimes feel that she is connected to the power of creation itself. The first flutters of movement will cause her eyes to widen in wonder, and, with time, the baby's movements within her will bring a smile of deep contentment. Her entire pregnancy will be a wonderful time of anticipation, during which she already begins the bonding that will last for the rest of her life. Today's woman may even see the image of her infant by ultrasound and have an even stronger bond to her child before birth.

The archetypal mother prefers natural childbirth if given the option. She wants to experience every second of the process to the fullest. She also wants to be in control of the birth and not give it over to medical personnel. Even for the woman who is not naturally of this archetypal nature, the first view of her new child is something she will never forget. For the archetypal mother, the first time she sees and holds her infant will be a profoundly religious experience in every sense of the word. She will feel herself touched by and in the presence of God. Her joy will, in those moments, be complete, and she will feel herself fulfilled. If possible, she will nurse her child as long as she is able, delighting in the physical sensation as well as the emotional satisfaction that it brings.

Rearing the child will be her joy. The realities of having to work, to arrange day care, and to send her child off to school will be very difficult for her. This is the woman today who feels such terrible guilt for not being home full time. If she can, she will make the sacrifices necessary to be at home. Like Demeter, she wants to spend her time with her youngsters, getting to know them and sharing the nurturing power of her love. In time, however, the child must grow up and begin his or her own life. The emotional separation may be devastating to the mother, even though she wants her child to be strong and independent as an adult. The process may seem like a thousand small deaths.

In the myth, the process of separation takes place violently. Persephone, the daughter, is raped and/or abducted by Hades, lord of the underworld, and is taken to his dark realm. Her mother, Demeter, learns that the god-king Zeus permitted the act and immediately goes to him for justice. En route, she is attacked and raped by Poseidon, lord of the sea. Finally, abused but not humiliated, she appears before Zeus and demands that he intervene. Zeus refuses, and so she returns to earth and takes matters into her own hands. Life gradually slows to a halt. The earth grows cold, plant life shrivels and dies, death's icy grasp threatens to choke the very breath out of creation. The Goddess refuses to hear the starving cries of earth's children; in her pain, she only feels the aching void of her own loss and the icy vengeance of her anger.

Finally, Zeus becomes frightened by the awesomely destructive power of her rage and agrees to intervene. He orders Hades to return the girl. But before Persephone returns, she eats a few seeds of a pomegranate, thus surrendering a piece of herself to her captor forever. Therefore, she returns to her mother for nine months of the year, the nine months of Demeter's fertility and creative abundance. During the other three months, she must return to Hades, and all the earth shivers in the shadow of winter's death until her return. Such is the power of a mother's rage and pain.

This second half of the myth graphically illustrates the agony of a mother who loses her child. Granted, not all daughters (or sons) leave their mothers' protection in such a cruel way. And the fact that both mother and daughter are raped and abused is more a comment on patriarchy than on the mother's feelings when a child leaves home. But the archetypal mother may still feel some of Demeter's despair.

Negative Energies of the Archetype

The dangerous energies of this archetype are the negative aspects of the mother's many positive strengths. In the first place, she may not wait until the appropriate time to become pregnant. If this happens, the archetype may have destructively taken over her life. Every young woman who feels the strong urge to have a baby needs to be very careful. She may need to protect herself against the time when she lets the archetype lead by getting some family planning counseling.

Once a woman does become a mother, she will need to beware that her love does not become possessive. The "smothering mother" may prevent the child from ever finding his or her own place in the world. Moreover, her child may have to pull away in a way that may deeply wound her. In her pain, she may become enraged at the child.

One woman who was dealing with painful feelings about separating from her own mother finally came to experience this in a dream. She dreamed that she was in the woods, a fairy-tale kind of forest, when she came upon a clearing. At its edge was a great brown bear, surrounded by cubs who were happily playing together under her watchful eye. The bear looked toward the woman, opened her arms, and invited her to come near. The woman slowly walked toward her, desperately wanting to lose herself in that warm, musky embrace. She said later that she felt a strangely primordial instinct to bury herself in the bear's fur, and to hide from the world in the safety of the bear's body. But as she drew near, the animal bared its great teeth and claws, and warned her, "If you enter, know that you will never leave. My love is so powerful that I would rather kill you than let you go."

The almost overwhelming love of an archetypal mother for her child may indeed be a very dangerous force if not kept within bounds. It can too easily become possessiveness, and that is a perverse distortion of love. A woman whose entire reason for living rests in her role of mother can feel terribly threatened and fearful as she sees that role coming to an end. Even when she knows intellectually that her greatest goal is to see her child become a responsible, independent adult, she emotionally wants to hang on for dear life.

Another side of possessiveness is jealousy. The archetypal mother may find herself jealous of her child's relationship with its father, and may subtly or not so subtly exclude him from the parenting role. Or she may be jealous of her child's friends and, eventually, lovers. The archetype of the interfering mother-in-law stems from this distortion of the mother's role. Retaining the love while releasing feelings of ownership may be a difficult challenge. The understanding that love will continue regardless of age or other significant relationships in the child's life may come only with time and experience.

While the child is at home, the greatest dangers for the mother may be these twin diseases of possessiveness and jealousy. Or they may be permissiveness and overgenerosity. It is very difficult for the archetypal mother to say "No." At least it is if she does not fully understand her role. Mothers who give their children everything they ask for are not doing them any favors.

Children do not learn to respect money or property until they have earned it themselves. Responsibility is only learned by practice. Encouraging youngsters to get jobs only to pay for luxuries and unnecessary electronic toys does not help, either. Youngsters should help to pay for their education, rather than their parents' using life insurance and second mortgages. Once the young person graduates, he or she should be immediately liable for his or her own living expenses: car, rent, utilities, food, insurance, etc. Paying for these new adults to live the same life-style as their parents does nothing to give them an awareness of reality.

The archetypal mother may have trouble with all of this. She may see it as her role to remortgage her house, borrow heavily against her insurance policies, and go deeply into debt for the sake of her child. Sacrifice is her middle name. Or, again, it may be if she does not understand her role better. Good mothering results in responsible children, not spoiled brats who become addicted consumers. This may be one of the most important things she will need to remember.

As dangerous as the temptations for the archetypal mother may be while her children are at home, the dangers may become even more intense when they do grow up and leave. The empty nest syndrome is usually expressed in jokes these days, especially now that many children are not leaving home until their mid-twenties. Mothers may be more inclined to push them out than to keep pulling them back in. But to many, the empty nest is not a joke at all.

Many women are now going through midlife divorces and changes in their careers. Community colleges, universities, even seminaries are full of them. Usually they juggle the demands of work, school, and single parenting very well. But there are other situations in which Mom must move to another city or state in order to attend school or to take a better job. Often, what happens in these instances is that the kids opt to stay home with Dad (and their peers) and send Mom out on her own.

I have talked with many of these women; I have been one of them myself. The circumstances vary, but we all agree that we have never been through more pain. For a woman who is an archetypal mother, it may well be too much. It is one thing to have your children move on to their new lives, but it is altogether different when, as mother, you leave them behind. The guilt and sense of loss can be overwhelming. Only time can teach us that love can continue long distance and that too much contact sometimes only produces friction.

What, then, does the archetypal mother do when she clears the nest? Some have a midlife baby; others become foster parents. Some use their nurturing skills in their career; some become volunteers or find new work that fits their needs better. Some wait patiently to turn their love toward grandchildren. All have vast stores of energy to invest. Their greatest danger is in letting loss and grief fill their days so that this archetypal energy goes unspent.

Sarah

The Bible is filled with stories about motherhood and birth. Several times in Scripture God intervenes and helps the creative process along. In the Hebrew culture, giving birth to sons was a woman's duty and joy. For most, it was the reason for which she was married and the purpose for which she lived. Women of sterile husbands fared as badly as those who were infertile because of their own physical problems since it was always assumed that the woman was at fault.

These so-called barren women were objects of both ridicule and scorn. The prayers of Rachel, Sarah, Hannah, and Elizabeth speak clearly to the pain of the archetypal mother who has no child. For the biblical women, the pain was sociological and financial as well as emotional. The loss of Naomi's sons left her and her daughters-in-law to seek another male relative's protection. Sons were social security and hope for comfortable old age. As heirs, sons carried the family property and name, an honor absolutely critical to a new nation's stability and growth.

Thus the mother's task was, quite literally, to provide the genetic continuation of her people. The more sons she bore, the more she was honored in the eyes of her family and her friends; the fewer she bore, the less honor she received. Now times have changed, but the desire for a son still remains strong for many women and men. "It's a boy!" has a very different sound to it than "It's a girl." The exclamation point is generally missing in the latter statement. Males still carry on the family name; females often give up their family names to adopt their husbands'. The preference for boys remains solidly with us. It is one of the culturally induced dangers of which the archetypal mothers of today will need to beware.

The twelve tribes of Israel are named for the sons and grandsons of Jacob, Rachel, Leah, Bilnah, and Zilpah. Jacob was born to Isaac and Rebecca. Isaac was the only son born to Abraham and Sarah. In the genealogy of the great patriarchs of Israel, the founding mother of them all was Sarah. As the one who first entered the promised land and who began the dynasty that would become a nation, she was the grand matriarch, the first mother of Israel. Thus her story is as important as it is powerful.

For almost all of her life, Sarah was childless, a condition that caused enormous pain to both her and her husband. But the pain was more than personal. They had heard a clear call from God to bear descendants. Maternity, to Sarah — as to all archetypal mothers — was felt as a divine call, a destiny that must be fulfilled if she was to be faithful. It was thus a matter of faith as much as biological or emotional urge. So it is for each of the archetypes: She is called to be a particular kind of woman in order to serve God in a particular way. For Sarah and millions of women since, this call was to motherhood.

The story of Abraham and Sarah is one of the most beloved in Scripture, a premier example of absolute faith and obedience to God. Through the experience of this one couple, the Hebrew people saw proof of God's promise to them as a race. They are not perfect human beings; in fact, Abram's treatment of Sarai is often deceitful and even horrifying in modern eyes. And yet that is not the primary importance of this epic tale; its importance centers around the birth of Isaac, whose life provided the proof that God's promises would come true.

The Child of Promise

Many years passed from the time that Sarai and Abram left their ancestral home until Isaac was finally born. Since Abram was said to be seventy-five when they left Haran and at least one hundred at Isaac's birth, it can be assumed that Sarai lived the span of a lifetime mourning her barren state. Scripture makes it clear that she was well beyond menopause when she miraculously conceived, whether their ages are inflated to show respect, as was often the case, or whether their ages are to be accepted as accurate.

The account of Isaac's conception helps to illustrate the overwhelming importance of his birth and of Sarai's fulfillment of her maternal call. Abram was promised very early in the tale (Gen. 12:7) that Yahweh would give the land of Canaan to his descendants. But an heir did not appear. Abram and Sarai journeyed to Egypt, where she was given to Pharaoh to save Abram's less-than-faithful neck. But God was on her side, and she was released to fulfill her task.

After receiving the blessing of Melchizedek, Abram met Yahweh once again and immediately challenged God with Sarai's failure to provide the promised son. He was assured that "no one but your very own issue shall be your heir." God took Abram outside the tent and said, "Look toward heaven and count the stars, if you are able to count them." Then God said to him, "So shall your descendants be" (Gen. 15:4–5). With this promise, the desire for a son becomes an issue of faith. But did Sarai hear it? We are not told.

Ten years later, no child had yet appeared, and the faith of the pair grew dim. When Sarai, following the custom of the day, offered her maid Hagar to Abram to be impregnated in her stead, the boy Ishmael was conceived. At last, Abram had a son! But Sarai did not. And apparently it was important to God that her role be fulfilled. Sarai's intuitive knowledge seemed to tell her that by following custom she had denied herself. Her rage was not directed against Yahweh or Abram. In the all-too-common way of confused women, it spilled out instead against Hagar.

This may be a warning to a woman who feels called to have a child. If she, for whatever reason, does not conceive, she may feel resentful or jealous of other women who do. The woman who wants a child but cannot have one or the woman who undergoes the difficult treatment for infertility often feels that the streets are filled with pregnant women. Young children and infants in strollers seem to be everywhere. Her mind and heart are so painfully sensitive to feelings of loss that she can only look with envy at those women who have what she does not. She may look at the large families of others, especially those who cannot adequately feed or care for them, and feel that a great injustice has been done. Where does she go with her anger? To God? To her husband, if she has one? Or to other women? Sometimes the latter seems the safest route, but it is a sad thing indeed when one woman oppresses another out of her own feelings of inadequacy. Yet this was the situation between Sarai and Hagar. The servant had accomplished what the wife had not.

Women today who are infertile sometimes try to find surrogate mothers to bear their husband's child. The court cases following some of these situations speak to the terrible difficulties of such a solution. Whether the kind of jealousy that Sarai felt for Hagar is a part of it is not usually discussed, but the surrogate still has to give up her child. Some may not even recognize the reality of the archetype within until the day of separation comes, and then it is too late.

Some women, especially young ones, give their babies up for adoption because they feel they are unable to care for them. They are convinced that it is the best thing to do for the welfare of the child, and they may be right. But I have seen the grief that can last for thirty and forty years afterward, and it is terrible indeed. Their anger, often directed toward the child's father, can be destructive as well.

Ishmael was born, but the promise was clearly not yet fulfilled. Then Yahweh appeared to Abram once again and renewed the covenant. The very first words of God in Genesis 17 state once more the promise of a great nation of heirs. Abram was renamed Abraham, "ancestor of a multitude"; Sarai became Sarah, "princess." God declared that she was to be the mother of the forthcoming race. Abraham's response was to fall on his face laughing (Gen. 17:17). God seemed to enjoy Abraham's response; the promised child, God said, would be named Isaac, "he laughs."

Immediately thereafter, in Genesis 18:1–15, the promise is given once again. Three men, later recognized as divine visitors, came to the couple's tent and received the customary hospitality of the day. They then repeated the covenant. This time Sarah heard them, too. Significantly, this appears to be the first time that she heard of her destiny from anyone other than her less-than-faithful husband (if, in fact, he had told her of it before). Her reaction? She too laughed (18:12). Out of fear? Joy? Disbelief? Gratitude? Relief? Probably all of the above. The promise had finally been received by the woman, and it was accepted.

The story should, perhaps end here. Abraham begat Isaac who begat Jacob who begat Reuben, Simeon, Levi, Judah, Zebulin, Issachar, Dan, Gad, Asher, Naphtali, Joseph, and Benjamin (not to mention daughters — they do not count in patriarchal lineage). Abraham is the great patriarch of Yahweh's chosen people; Sarah the unmentioned mother of nations. Motherhood fulfilled divine promise and human longing. Sarah fulfilled her function. Isaac was conceived and born. Once again Sarah drove Hagar and her son out, and this time Yahweh let them go under divine protection, back to her country and her people.

The Final Test

After these things, God tested Abraham: "Abraham!" And Abraham answered, "Here I am." God said, "Take your son, your only son Isaac, whom you love, and go to the land of Moriah, and offer him there as a burnt offering on one of the mountains that I shall show you" (Gen. 22:1–2). The rest of the story is well known.

But what of Sarah? What of the mother? What of the woman who had been given by her husband to two other men in order to save his own skin? What of the barren woman who gave her slave to have the child she so desperately wanted? What of the woman to whom the angels had promised a son, in fact, as many descendants as the stars in the skies? What did she feel as her husband left with two other men, her beloved child, and an ass loaded with kindling? What about her faith in her husband — and in a God who would demand such a thing?

Several years ago at a meeting of church women that I attended, the story of Sarah was presented in interpretive dance. All of her beauty, her early hopefulness, her wifely submissiveness, and even her gradual aging came alive. Her terrible jealousy of Hagar and her despair at her own barrenness were painfully enacted. The dancer's portrayal of the agonizingly long ordeal of the old woman's giving birth held the audience in spell-bound silence. And then Sarah's pride and delight and joy were uncontainable. Every mother there was brought back to the sight of her own first-born child, to the sacred, profound, and wonderful mystery of birth.

But, again, the story did not stop there. Sarah watched in horror as Abraham took away her son, her life, her purpose on earth. Once again, however, she was obedient. And, as five hundred women watched, the beautiful body on stage was ravaged by grief. Abraham returned with Isaac unharmed, but Sarah was broken, destroyed. She was Abraham's actual sacrifice. She had been obedient once too often.

Integration for Today's Mother

The archetypal mother of today feels as strongly as Sarah the desire to give birth. Her reaction to pregnancy may be the same as well. Although Sarah's laughter was ambiguous in meaning, there is no ambiguity at all in the joy of an archetypal mother who conceives for the first time. Pregnancy, birthing, nursing, and all aspects of rearing a child will bring joy. Her own innate strengths will usually tell her what to do in any given situation. She will gladly give of herself for the well-being of her child.

The positive side of the archetype is clear and may be enjoyed by any woman. If biological motherhood is impossible, a woman may choose adoption or foster parenthood. Either provides fulfillment for such women and offers exceptional mothering to children who might otherwise have little or none. Beyond the actual rearing of children, the archetypal mother's innate selflessness, generosity, nurturing, and caregiving capabilities can be utilized in various situations. Women with such God-given skills fill many types of social service roles, and there is a great need for more such women.

The joys of being mother to a child, whether by biology or adoption, have been portrayed in so many ways by so many storytellers and artists that it would be impossible to reduce them to a page. The mother's strengths, though, can be roughly identified as those that bring up a child to be a joyful, responsible adult.

Sometimes, however, we dwell too much on the responsibilities. Sarah's laughter may alert us to another aspect of motherhood. A mother's own joy as she lives out what she feels to be her calling from God will be passed on to her child. The sheer delight in being who she is can transmit to a child pride in self and optimism toward the future. A mother's attitude toward herself as a woman will help to shape the child's feelings toward females, and a mother's self-love will help promote self-love in her child.

The dangers, however, are there as well. Integration for a woman whose archetypal nature is maternal will mean consciously expanding her role beyond the home into other areas of life beside her children. Putting all of her energies into her own family may not be healthy for her or for them. She will need to intentionally cultivate the strengths of one of the three independent archetypes in preparation for the time when her children are grown. The greatest threat to her personal fulfillment may be in trying to live her life through them instead of letting them go when they must. It is one thing for a woman to derive enjoyment and fulfillment from having and rearing children; it is another to hold them so closely that they feel they must carry responsibility for her reality for the rest of their lives.

The archetypal mother will also need to be as responsible for *herself* as she feels for them. One of her greatest challenges may be to mother herself. Women are often not very good at taking care of themselves. We are too well programmed to give ourselves to and for others, but mothering ourselves, offering ourselves the love and care that we give our kids, might be enormously beneficial. It may be even more important for the woman who does not or cannot have children.

Those of us who have children seem to spend an inordinate amount of time seeing that they have enough rest, exercise, and good food. We make sure they brush their teeth, take their vitamins, wear their boots. We read books to them, send them to school, and give them educational games. We encourage them to be creative, and we watch that their friends are as positive and strong as we want our youngsters to be. All of these are healthy ways of using one's maternal energies.

But what about ourselves? Whether we have children or not, it is vital that we mother ourselves in the same ways. We can check to make sure that we are eating properly and getting enough rest and exercise. We can take our own vitamins and practice preventative medicine for ourselves. We can go back to school, take extension courses, or attend workshops. We can take the time to read a good novel from time to time. We can discover and exercise our own creative talents, and we can go out of our way to cultivate and then to spend time with good friends.

When we are feeling low, we can sit in a rocking chair and hold ourselves. One single woman I know has a stuffed animal that she hugs. Sometimes the stuffed animal represents herself that she holds and rocks, and sometimes it takes the place of a child. But she finds enormous solace in it. And as she says, "Bear" never talks back or messes up clothes or rooms. Mothering ourselves may be the most important use of the archetype's energies.

One more major focus for the archetypal mother, though, will be the letting go. Any mother whose children are gone knows the anguish of their loss. It is like going through childbirth all over again, releasing them to set them free. However, it is always helpful to remember that, like Hagar and Ishmael, we can send them out with the prayerful protection and knowledge of God. Our responsibility is not only to help build a healthy body and mind. It is also to feed and nourish our children with the love of God so that they may mature in faith as they mature in years.

This we cannot do if we are unaware of our own God-given worth as women created in the divine image. If we allow ourselves to be abused by our husbands or the social order as Sarah was, we are teaching our children messages of injustice and oppression. Only if we feel good about ourselves, can we really transmit a healthy attitude about women and about the God who created us to be what we are.

Motherhood is sacred. It is a holy calling and a divine gift. For me, there is no experience on earth more miraculous than feeling life move within one's own body, and then seeing that life for the first time after the trauma of giving birth. Surely, it must be at least something like God's all embracing love for each of us, for we are God's children every bit as much as our infants are ours. And God must beam with pride at our first steps, first words, first teeth. But God must also weep at our disastrous choices and arrogant ways. God knows the joys and pains of motherhood. God had an only child, and yet, even after we did what we did to him, God forgives, and loves, and offers us yet one more chance. Perhaps we, too, can learn to be mothers who accept both joy and pain, who are compassionate and forgiving, and who will release our children to bring others God's peace.

Questions for Reflection

Motherhood is an extremely complex symbol. It is very difficult to release our personal preconceptions, but for our own spiritual as well as psychological well being, we need to try. Perhaps these questions may help to add some new dimensions to our old understanding, or perhaps they may even help replace our outdated images with new.

1. If you have children, what are your greatest maternal gifts? Your greatest joys?

2. If you have never had a child, how do you use your healthy "mothering" capabilities?

3. Who are you other than "mother"? In what way do you need your children (or your mothering-type job) for your identity?

4. Have you "let go" appropriately? How can you show your love without doing too much?

5. Do you mother yourself? How?

6. Are you comfortable with maternal images of God? Of Christ? If not, what makes you uncomfortable?

CHAPTER SEVEN

The Daughter

We have looked at various types of women in their relationships and their roles. Now, we look at an archetypal reality that belongs to all women regardless of the type of their relationship or role. We are all daughters. Some may say, "Yes, but I've outgrown that category. Now I am an independent woman, a wife, a mother, even a grandmother." Others may never have known their biological parents, and some have had a number of parenting figures.

Regardless of what occurs after our birth, we spend much of our lives working out the psychological legacy from our parents whether we know them or not. It is the entire psychological journey that in fact defines the archetypal daughter. Her story is one of process and maturation, movement and growth. It includes three stages of a woman's life: her early years as a dependent child, her early adult life of choice and increased vulnerability to the world, and her mature role as wise mentor and guide.

The daughter, then, speaks to us of ourselves — past, present, and future. She speaks to us of pilgrimage and of journey. She speaks psychologically of integration and wholeness, completion and maturity. She also speaks to us spiritually of faith, hope, and healing.

Mother and Daughter in Myth

Mythologically, this process has been well understood for thousands of years. It has been repeated in one culture after another in the myths of Ishtar, Inanna, Psyche, Proserpina, and Persephone. Although there are differences between the various stories, the journey is much the same. It is a woman's coming of age. In the very earliest myths, mother and daughter are one. The woman (the Goddess) is at one within herself and with the created order. In psychological terms, there is an undifferentiated fusion that exists as her first state of being.

Then a decision is made to enter the netherworld, the dark place of the dead. Here she suffers unspeakable torment as she experiences both the death of her innocent self and the birth of her new responsible being. This painful transformation is the second phase of her journey.

Finally, she returns to earth — but not as the same person she was. Now she must learn to live with the pain, anger, and sorrow that have entered her soul. Slowly, acceptance and integration come, until she is the wise woman of maturity who acts as spiritual guide to others who must also undergo the descent into hell. The Bible picks up this same theme when Adam and Eve are cast out of the garden, east of Eden.

Perhaps the most well-known of these mythological Goddesses is Persephone, daughter of the earth mother Demeter. Ancient sources tell us Persephone was abducted and/or raped by Hades, lord of the underworld, and taken forcibly to be his wife. As we have seen, her mother felt the girl's loss as the loss of her very self and went to Zeus to demand justice. En route, she too was brutally raped. When she finally appeared before Zeus, he refused to hear her complaint. In her pain and sorrow, she withdrew into an icy rage, and life on earth slowly ground to a halt.

Meanwhile, beneath the earth, Persephone languished in depression and grief. Finally, Zeus became frightened at the power of Demeter's rage and ordered the daughter to be released. But what was done could not be undone; virginity can never be restored. Persephone ate a few seeds of the pomegranate, the fruit of passion, and therefore was required to spend three months of each year with Hades in his dark kingdom. She returned to Demeter bringing springtime with her, but the cycle could never again be stopped.

There was a difference, however. When Persephone stepped back into the world of darkness, she did so as a mature queen and no longer as a victimized daughter. She had grown up.

A woman's psychological journey is much like this. We grow up as virginal young girls, daughters of our mothers, often not knowing where one leaves off and the other begins. Then something happens. We lose our innocence. We leave our mother's sphere of protection and venture out into the world.

For many, the second stage of our journey begins as we first experience the world of our sexuality. The loss of our virginity is always a major event in our lives whether it is a joyful decision or something much more painful. For many women, it marks the end of the first part of our life, our life as a daughter. We now no longer belong to our mothers but enter the dangerous and oft-times painful realm of men. We are on our own.

Even if there is no physical loss of virginity, a woman must at some point leave her mother's house and become her own person. This is the expansion of our network that Carol Gilligan identifies as the second phase of women's psychological development. We must find our own place in the world and suffer all the ills, pains, and sorrows the world has to offer. This second part of the archetypal journey often becomes very difficult, at times even traumatic. After time and experience, however, we begin to heal. The broken pieces come together and an integrated whole begins to form. We, too, like Persephone, can become a queen.

Negative Energies of the Archetype

This, then, is the journey of the archetypal daughter. She is more than young girl, although that is her beginning. One danger is that she may remain a psychological child. Some women, due to deep emotional scars left from childhood are never quite able to mature into the adults they were created to be. They may need a great deal of love and prayer to be healed of their past.

Statistics are now telling us that at least one out of every three women and men in this country are victims of some kind of childhood sexual violence. Although incest and sexual violation of young children are finally beginning to be documented and recognized as the serious epidemic that they are, we are still a long way from being able to do much for the survivors. Twelve-step programs, combined with professional counseling, seem to be providing the best possibilities, but the trauma suffered will never fully leave. Emotionally, the daughter may remain trapped in her little girl's terror, unwarranted guilt, and shame.

Like sexual abuse, most of the dangers of this stage of the daughter's archetypal journey are not due to her own error. More likely, they come from something beyond her control. Negative energies from outside her psyche can afflict and oppress her until her journey is rerouted onto a less healthy and positive track. Insufficient or inadequate parenting, poverty and all of its evils, physical or mental disabilities — all of these are early challenges that may permanently affect the young girl. Or they may provide an impetus for her to survive and thrive. The remainder of her journey will tell which path she takes.

The middle part of the daughter's life has its own pitfalls and dangers, as the myth makes abundantly clear. This is often a time of intense pain, suffering, and loss. Most women do not find the negative aspects of adulthood overwhelming and also find more than adequate pleasures to offset the pain. But the possibilities for suffering are real and cannot be overlooked. In the earliest myths, the woman makes her own choice to enter the underworld. At least she is given the dignity of having made the decision herself. Only after patriarchy succeeded Goddess worship did the myths begin to include rape and forcible abduction.

Today's daughter growing up may take either route. Whichever path she takes, she will be vulnerable to all that the social order has to offer, both good and bad. Her task and her challenge will be to grow through her experiences and not to become lost in them. The major danger for the archetype at this point is losing her way and remaining in her own psychological hell. It may be that this is the most critical time of her passage, and where her faith becomes critical. Her ability to walk through the valley of the shadow may well depend on the spiritual guide(s) she invites to help her.

Finally, if she has made it through the darkness, the archetypal journey is completed in triumph. Now the whitewaters of earlier times smooth out. Or, maybe she simply begins to sit back and enjoy the ride since she has learned the necessary survival skills to make it through. In any event, her hard-won expertise becomes a valuable nugget of wisdom that she can share with others who are on the way. She has become integrated, complete, and whole.

Mary of Nazareth

We have few examples in Scripture showing the entire journey of a woman's life. Perhaps the fullest and the most powerful account we have of an archetypal daughter's passage to maturity and wisdom is that of Mary of Nazareth. In Mary's story, a woman's pilgrimage can be seen in all of its joy and beauty, suffering and loss. She grows from the virginal daughter to one who suffers the agonies of hell to the mature queen of heaven, spiritual guide of the faithful. She also expands the archetypal image from that of a woman's psychological journey to that of a spiritual pilgrimage. Mary was more than a daughter; she was the daughter of God.

Reverence for Mary has been part of the Christian faith from the early church. The Council of Ephesus in 432 defined her as *Theotokos*, Mother of God. She has always been a focus of what we might call "folk piety." Many people in the early years of the church found in Mary a gentle, approachable maturity to which they could relate. Moreover, such devotion became even stronger as the centuries progressed.

By the Middle Ages, Christianity had become largely a cult of the priests. Worshipers could hardly understand the language of the Mass; by the twelfth century the communion wine was reserved for priests only; few believers were literate or had access to the Bible.

Christianity became magical and superstitious as the common folk lost their sense of connection with symbol and ritual. They felt a deep need and yearning to be connected, as all of us do, to be intimately engaged, involved in the faith, to be relationally touched by God.

For these reasons, reverence for Mary slowly evolved into a worship of Mary. She, at least, was real, warm, human. She was the mother of mothers, and she was the mother of sons. She had been through hell and had suffered as many of them suffered. She understood, they felt, in ways that even Jesus could not understand. Mary was fully human, flesh and blood, real.

Yet, she was also pure and undefiled, as they were not. She had not been tainted by the world. Even in her agonizing sorrow, she was not embittered, enraged, or broken in defeat. Mary became a symbol of hope, a virginal presence that took one away from the dingy realities of this world. Her body was always pure and untouched, even by death. Paintings of her bodily ascension assured her followers that there was not even physical decay. She was and is ever virgin, ever pure.

In this, she provided the faithful an alternative to their own lives. In prayers to her, they could feel purity touch them. She became more than mediator; she ofttimes became the healer. Visions of her changed people's lives. Shrines were erected in places where she was said to have visited, and the sick and troubled would take long and often difficult pilgrimages to be in the place where she had been seen, to pray at the shrine of her presence, and to be healed. Many have been and still are touched by divine grace at these places.

Finally, in 1854, Pope Pius IX promulgated the dogma of the Immaculate Conception, which concluded that Mary was, indeed, more than human; that she, like her son, was born without sin. Mary was thereby considered to be both the natural daughter of Anna and her husband Joachim and the supernatural daughter of God. According to Carl Jung, the papal pronouncement elevated Mary to equal status with the Trinity. Indeed, Jung concluded joyfully, at last there was quadernity (he considered four the perfect number). More importantly, he believed, the feminine was finally given its due and elevated to the divinity it once had and always deserved.

One more word needs to be spoken about Christian history

and the mother of Jesus, the daughter of God. During the Protestant Reformation in the sixteenth century worship of Mary had become, in the eyes of some, idolatry. For this reason, in an attempt to correct all of the abuses of the church and return the worship of God to the people, Mary was not-so-gently put completely out of sight and mind. Protestants, therefore, were left no feminine symbols at all: no Mary, no female saints, no nuns. God is identified as male, Jesus Christ is male, even the Holy Spirit is often referred to as male. Christian doctrine has become as intellectually and frigidly masculine as early matrifocal culture was emotionally and sensually feminine. Perhaps, however, there might be a place for both/and. Perhaps we can find a way back that celebrates both the divine masculine and the divine feminine. And, in terms of a woman's spiritual and psychological journey, perhaps she can once again claim her own God-given power as one born in the image of her Creator.

Let us take another look at Mary, daughter of God and mother of Jesus, for it is her journey that helps us recognize the wholeness of our own pilgrimage. Her path gives our own journey shape, direction, and purpose. It also helps us perceive the centrality of Jesus Christ in our lives, even as he was in hers.

Mary of Nazareth, daughter of Joachim and Anna, is first described by tradition as a young Jewish girl from a small town in the Palestinian outback of Galilee. Like all good Jewish girls, she would have been docile, submissive, and obedient to her earthly parents' wishes. Thus when she was of marriageable age, about fourteen, and her parents promised her to a man many years her elder, she accepted their decision. In all actuality, she had no choice. Here was a "Persephone-type" in all her youth and innocence living with her parents as the obedient child and preparing to enter marriage as the equally submissive wife.

But then something happened. Was the coming of the Holy Spirit another Hades-type instance of divine rape? Or, was Mary allowed the integrity of making a personal decision, as in the prepatriarchal accounts of the Persephone myth? It would seem that God is considerably more honorable than men and other gods, for Mary was approached with respect by the holy messenger. When she heard the words of promise, she responded as a person with rights. She asked for an explanation, and when it was given to her satisfaction, she made her decision with a personal commitment. This was no rape, nor was there blind, passive submission. In this act, God restored to all women — through Mary — the value of our own integrity.

Mary's volitional act is important for understanding the archetypal daughter. Some young women will come to the end of the first part of their journey and merely let circumstances take their course. They will not accept responsibility nor be accountable for what happens next. It is also true that some are not given the option. But most of us, at least in this country, do have choices. We must decide whether to continue school or go directly to work. Whether to marry is a critical decision; whom to marry is even more so. We need to decide whether to start our family immediately or to wait until we have become established in a career.

Mary of Nazareth may not have had all of our options because of the religious and social law of her day, but God returned to her the power of her own decision. Perhaps in these very first steps of her journey we can begin to discern the other side of the archetypal daughter, the archetypal daughter of God. Even though she was bound by cultural norms, God gave her the freedom to decide her future for herself. So we may have options we do not think possible. If we accept our role as daughters of God, our worth and identity takes on a whole new meaning, and we, too, may receive back the integrity we thought we had lost.

Mary's sheltered life as Anna and Joachim's daughter came to an abrupt halt with her betrothal and conception. From the time of the annunciation, her life was radically altered. She was suddenly outside of social convention: a pregnant, unwed teenager. Her fiance seriously considered ending the engagement, and it again took divine intervention to convince him to go through with the wedding (Matt. 1:19–25). The Gospel writers do not tell us of Anna and Joachim's response to her pregnancy, and it may be unfair to conjecture. Pious tradition that led to the Immaculate Conception dogma would insist that they fully knew and understood.

But Mary, at least according to the Lukan sources, chose to leave home for a three-month visit to her older cousin, Elizabeth. On this visit, she exclaimed the incredible words known as the Magnificat (Luke 1:46–55) that so beautifully foretell Jesus' mission. That the words are divinely inspired is clear; that they came from the mouth of an adolescent girl should be astonishing. But then, Jesus' mission, even as Mary describes it to Elizabeth, was astonishing. He came to turn the "natural" order upside down, and at least one part of this upheaval was clearly to return to women the power that was theirs at creation.

After three months, just before Elizabeth gave birth to John, Mary returned home to her fiance. Before the wedding was celebrated, according to Luke, Joseph was called to Bethlehem as a member of the family of David in order to be counted in a census. Mary, close to term, went with him. The ninety-mile walk — or donkey ride — would have been excruciating, and it appears to have brought on her labor.

We now have such blissful pictures of the radiant madonna deeply implanted in our consciousness that it is hard to imagine or consider Mary's real condition. Her pregnancy had not been easy. She was unmarried, she hardly knew her fiance, she spent her first trimester with an older cousin — perhaps because of the derision and gossip back home. She then had to, or chose to, undertake an extremely uncomfortable ride to a strange city with this man whom she barely knew and to whom, according to Luke, she had not yet been married. Finally, she had to accept him as her only attendant during this, her first birth.

We are accustomed to visualizing Mary serenely smiling at the pink and white infant as shepherds and kings, animals and angels worship on bended knee. But let us be fair to Mary's humanity for a change. Giving birth to a first child is agonizing, as all of us who have been through this experience know. It is often terrifying, and it is always traumatic. There was no woman there to explain to her what was happening, to calm her fears, to assure her that her incredible pain was normal. There was no one but her fiance to reach between her legs and guide forth the bloody infant, to cut the cord, to deliver and dispose of the afterbirth.

Yes, it was a miracle. Yes, it would cause angels to sing. Yes, it was a pivotal moment in human history. But, for Mary, it was totally, humanly, painfully, frightfully, traumatically real.

According to Luke, the couple soon went to Jerusalem to have the baby dedicated at the temple; in Matthew they fled to Egypt to escape King Herod. Whichever was the case, Mary was moving farther and farther from her parents' protection. She had left innocence far behind and was well on her way to her experience of a descent into the underworld. She would never again be the innocent daughter; she must now accept the responsibilities of wife and mother. She had entered the second stage of her life and must face all the pain and uncertainty of it. In a word, she must grow up.

Our own moving away from home may not be as difficult as Mary's, but it is also a distinct change of life. The decisions we face begin to have more and more serious consequences, and the skills we must develop in terms of marriage, career, and family seem to be overwhelming. Even if we only move across town, our journey may seem as long and difficult as hers as we make the change from little girl to adult.

We hear nothing more of the family for twelve years in Luke, thirty in Matthew. The Lukan account tells the strange story of Jesus, just come of age, staying behind at the temple during the family's annual pilgrimage at Passover. His parents did not miss him; he did not inform them of his decision. But Luke uses this story to insert the first disruptive element in the narrative since the strange story of his conception and birth: Jesus renounces his biological parents and states his primary heritage as God's child. It is a theme repeated again and again.

We have heard it so often that we nod our heads and agree without thinking: Son of man, Son of God, spiritual conception, divine and human. But there is more than this. What of Mary? What did Jesus do by renouncing her?

Again and again in Scripture we hear Jesus make the same outrageous statements. His first miracle, according to John, took place at Cana (John 2:1–11). During the wedding feast, Mary noticed the wine running low and spoke to Jesus about it. It is strange that Mary expected Jesus to do something about it; providing the wine would have been the wedding steward's responsibility. Jesus' answer is stranger still: "Woman, what concern is that to you and to me. My hour has not yet come" (2:4). Yet the miracle happens. Is this, perhaps, an example of a young man's necessary individuation from his mother? Her concerns are indeed no longer his. He is about God's business.

Jesus and the Family

The Christian faith has touted family values for centuries. American Christianity, in fact, has virtually turned the so-called nuclear family into a political mandate. But Jesus makes some truly bizarre statements about the biological family. When Mary brings her other children to find Jesus and take him home, thinking him deranged (Matt. 12:46–50; Mark 3:31–35; Luke 8:19–21), he refuses even to see them. In all three accounts, although the words vary slightly, the response is "Who are my mother and my brothers? . . . Whoever does the will of God is my brother and sister and mother" (Mark 3:33, 35). We may spiritualize these words, and we most often do, but it may also be that Jesus spoke them very literally. The Christian family is not based on biology; it is based on faith.

On another occasion a woman joyfully exclaimed, "Blessed is the womb that bore you and the breasts that nursed you!" Jesus replied, "Blessed rather are those who hear the word of God and obey it" (Luke 11:27–28). What does this say about motherhood? Are we biologically determined? Biologically identified?

What is Jesus saying about family?

> Do not think that I have come to being peace to the earth; I have not come to bring peace, but a sword.
>> For I have come to set a man against his father,
>>> and a daughter against her mother,
>> and a daughter-in-law against her mother-in-law;
>>> and one's foes will be members of one's own household.
>>> (Matt. 10:34–36)

Or again, Luke 12:52–53:

> Do you think that I have come to bring peace to the earth? No, I tell you, but rather division! From now on five in one household will be divided, three against two and two against three; they will be divided:
>> father against son
>>> and son against father,
>> mother against daughter
>>> and daughter against mother,
>> mother-in-law against her daughter-in-law
>>> and daughter-in-law against her mother-in-law.
>>> (Luke 12:52–53)

Or in Luke 14:26–27: "Whoever comes to me and does not hate father and mother, wife and children, brothers and sisters, yes, and even life itself, cannot be my disciple." Or again in Matthew 10:37–38: "Whoever loves father or mother more than me is not worthy of me; and whoever loves son or daughter more than me is not worthy of me." Or Matthew 19:29–30 (see Mark 10:29–30; Luke 18:29–30): "And everyone who has left houses or brothers or sisters or father or mother or children or fields, for my name's sake, will receive a hundredfold, and will inherit eternal life." In the last days Jesus predicted that "brother will betray brother to death, and a father his child, and children will rise against parents and have them put to death" (Matt. 10:21).

Is Jesus against the family? Of course not. But he is making a radical statement about the purpose of families. Families are not holy unto themselves. Put another way, families are not inherently valuable. There is no place in the Christian gospel for idolatry of the family. The worth of families comes only insofar as they are faithful to Jesus' message of global justice and peace. Families focused only on themselves and their own security are not families at all in the sight of God.

The parentage of Christians is divine; our genetic imprint is that of the imago Dei. Therefore, we are not called to be psychological clones of our biological parents but to grow into the Christlikeness that is our inheritance and spiritual encoding from God.

What does this say to women? What must this message have meant to Mary? It must have been terribly painful for her to hear such radical and seemingly derogatory statements about the family. The wonderful and incredible part of the story is that Mary stayed, suffered the pain and confusion of her own soul, and listened. Once again, she made the decision to enter the darkness. She chose to follow; she chose to become whole.

The dangers of the archetypal journey to maturation include the very strong possibility that we will simply give up. Jesus' teachings are not easy. His "hard sayings" were difficult for many to hear. Even devoted followers misunderstood him time and time again. As often as he forewarned his disciples about his coming death, they could — or would — not accept it. When the time came, almost all of them forgot his words and ran away.

But not the women. Not Mary. She watched the whole horrible process of her son's crucifixion. There are no words to describe her experience. Artists have made the attempt, but even they cannot know, much less portray, the kind of agony she endured. How many of us can even consider putting our own children in Jesus' place? I cannot. It is too horrible. My mind refuses to imagine it. I could not, I feel, survive such an ordeal — even in my imagination.

Mary, however, did survive. She followed her son every step of the way, and when he was dying a humiliating, agonizing death, she remained close enough to hear him. "When Jesus saw his mother and the disciple whom he loved standing beside her, he said to his mother, 'Woman, here is your son.' Then he said to the disciple, 'Here is your mother.' And from that hour the disciple took her into his own home" (John 19:26–27).

We read those words and put them into some homey, sentimental context of Jesus' seeing to it that his poor little mother will have a man once again to look after her. But Mary had other children. The people of Nazareth had asked: "Is not this the carpenter, the son of Mary and brother of James and Joses and Judas and Simon, and are not his sisters here with us?" (Mark 6:3–4). In fact, brother James became the first bishop of the church in Jerusalem. As the second eldest, it would have been his responsibility to take care of their mother.

And what of John, the beloved disciple? The son of Zebedee already had a mother who had, in fact, been present through most of Jesus' ministry. Salome had even requested of Jesus that her sons James and John be given special status in the Kingdom. Did John really need another mother?

No, something else is going on here. The real power of Mary's story resides, it seems to me, in this new mature understanding of family. This is the message behind Mary's journey, and the wisdom that she gained as an archetypal daughter of God.

All through his ministry, Jesus told us that the children we are to care for are the sick and the starving. Yes, he loves our clean, warm, well-fed, educated kids, but he wants us to provide the same sanitation, shelter, food, clothes, and education for the children of the Sudan. Or the urban ghetto. Or the other side of the tracks in our small town. Or the 17 percent of American children who live in poverty. Or the 9 percent of American children who are homeless.

For Jesus, motherhood means giving birth and nurturing one's young, yes, but it also means ensuring that mothers around the world are healthy enough to nurse their babies too, that the mothers on our streets find adequate housing, child care, and jobs. Jesus had four brothers and several sisters in his nuclear family, but he has millions of brothers and sisters who claim to follow him in faith. In order to be faithful to this call, they need the wisdom that his mother learned.

Mary's story is the story of letting go in order to grow up. This may well be the archetypal journey all of us must follow. She learned that although being a wife and mother may be a divine gift, it cannot provide all of the answers of being for a woman's life. She must, as the old adage says, "Let go and let God." She needs to release her biological family and, with Jesus, embrace all of humankind.

What Jesus seems to be telling us through his mother is that we will only reach our maturity when we accept responsibility for all of the starving, lonely people in God's world. Bringing up our own children is only the beginning. Our divine call as mature daughters of God is to feed, clothe, and provide shelter to those of God's family who are in need. This is the only way we will grow up to be mature Christians and mature human beings.

As Mary joined the disciples in the upper room, she ended the second part of her journey and stood on the brink of the third. Her understanding of mission to the hungry and the weak, spoken first as a pregnant teenager at the door of her older cousin, found its way into the very foundations of the Christian church. Her journey was fulfilled.

Integration for Today's Daughter

We are all too aware of the usual therapeutic processes of taking a troubled person back to their family of origin in order to ferret out the hows, whats, and whys of their particular psychological pathology. Mary's story as the archetypal daughter of God gives us another opportunity for healing as well. For many people, releasing our biological parents and looking instead toward the divine Parent of us all may set us free from a lot of past emotional garbage.

As helpful as psychology can be, troubled Christians also have the immense resources of our faith to aid in our recovery. There might even be a greater possibility for forgiving abusive or neglectful parents if we can feel assured of One who has been loving, caring, and weeping for us from the very first moment of our lives. We are daughters of God just as Mary was.

Being daughters of God, we are also given the option of choice. We can claim sovereignty over our lives. It may not be easy, but the journey to maturity never is. Whether we are more the fathers' daughter, the sister, the wise one, the wife, the mother, or the daughter, we are responsible for our own lives. God may offer us options, but it is up to us to accept. Unlike the gods of the Greek pantheon, our God does not abuse and rape. Rather, in accepting our creation in the divine image, we receive back the integrity that the social order tries to take away. What does Mary's story say to the archetypal mother about letting go of children? If there was any woman identified by giving birth, it was Mary of Nazareth. Yet from her son's twelfth birthday, this relationship was denied. If we accept twelve as the age of maturity, as the Hebrew people believed it to be, the message is clear: We cannot hold onto our children too long — psychologically or physically. Like Mary, we may have to learn to stand back and let them stand on their own two feet — or to fall on their face without catching them on the way down. Does that sound harsh? Psychologists call it "tough love." If we stop romanticizing Scripture, the message is nothing less.

The most we can do, especially as mothers, is to give our children the opportunity of faith. We cannot give them faith; only God can do that. But we can see that they are exposed to the great stories, rituals, prayers, hymns, creeds, and history of our tradition. We can be examples of people who accept responsibility for ourselves. We cannot be doormats to our husbands, our bosses, or our kids. We need to set rules and boundaries, and stick to them. Denying our own self-worth provides a terrible example to both our daughters and our sons. Accepting the challenges and difficulties of this world offers a much healthier view to them of what God intended. Look to Mary, daughter of God, and take to heart the road she chose to follow.

Mary's story is archetypal of our own in many, many ways. She is far more than mother, although that was the vehicle by which she traveled her particular road to maturity. First, she provides an archetypal image of a woman's journey to psychological maturity. We see her first as an innocent virgin. Her first years of marriage were, by any account, traumatic. Her eldest son began his denial of her at age twelve, and publicly repeated it time and time again. Her older husband died, and she experienced the wrenching agony of widowhood, possibly of being a single mother. Finally, Jesus was crucified as a common criminal. She was told not to stay with one of her other sons, but with an unrelated man. Hers was surely a journey through her own personal hell.

She was not left at the foot of the cross, however, nor did she run away. Her final place was not even as John's "responsibility"; rather, she is last mentioned waiting in the upper room with the other disciples for the Holy Spirit she knew would come. She experienced herself as a complete woman: sexually, emotionally, mentally, socially, and spiritually. She accepted responsibility for her actions and made difficult and painful decisions. Mary regained the sovereignty over her life that Sarah never had and that Eve lost.

Second, Mary is the archetypal image of every woman's spiritual pilgrimage. As she moved from innocence through darkness into wisdom, she followed the only path that would light her way. All Christians profess that they follow Jesus Christ and him alone. Women must love him more than mother, father, sister, brother, lover, husband, or child, or they are idolaters. This is the painful but powerful message Mary offers to us all.

Our journey will undoubtedly bring pain as well as pleasure, suffering as well as joy. But keeping our eyes focused on God brings transformation through even the darkest of times. What we may need to remember is that wholeness does not come from our parents, our lovers, our husbands, or our children. Nor does our identity. Nor does our worth. Nor can we give our sovereignty over to these others.

Mary was not left hopeless and helpless when Jesus died. She was by then a woman strong enough to endure the worst life had to offer. Instead of giving up, or letting grief consume her, she was last seen surrounded by a community of faith awaiting the coming of God's Spirit with power. And since that time, she has become a beacon of hope for millions of Christians around the world.

Thus Mary provides an archetypal image for the churches.

Jesus' family did transcend biology. His call to discipleship was an invitation to be full participants in God's family: the family not only of fellow believers but of all of humankind. Those who believe, who know that they are children of God, are merely instructed to tell the rest of creation the same Good News. Committed Christians who make up Christ's church are to go out as sisters and brothers, fathers and mothers to the poor, the lonely, the sick, and the oppressed. We are to treat them as family — for they are our family — and to supply them with the good things we would supply to our own parents or children.

The church, like Mary, is called to be a daughter — and a mother — of God, sent into the world to give birth to a whole new order.

Questions for Reflection

There are many ways we can meditate on Mary's story. We can look to her in our psychological journey. We can seek to follow her in our spiritual journey. We can also look to her as an example for the church. Our difficulty may be in trying to relate to her at all. Over the years Mary's humanity has been so often denied that it is difficult for some of us to think of her as another living, breathing, joyful, sexual, suffering person. It is hard to think of her as a daughter, like ourselves, much less as another woman. And when we consider her womanhood, we may think that her grief was so profound that we dare not come near her with our own. And yet that is her gift. She offers us her pain as the golden road by which our own can be healed. By following in her steps, we, too, can become whole.

1. *When was the time of your innocence? Has it ended? Why? How?*

2. *When did you descend into your own personal hell? Has it ended? When? How?*

3. *Have you psychologically let go of your parents and/ or children and trusted them into God's care? If not, what is holding you back?*

4. *How do you relate to Mary of Nazareth as the daughter of God? In what ways can you identify with her journey to wholeness?*

5. *How do you understand yourself as a daughter of God? Is this understanding based on your own family or on God's family?*

6. *What is your connection with the parents and children who are starving and homeless in your own world or globally?*

PART
FOUR

IMAGE

CHAPTER EIGHT

The Catalyst

D ictionaries define a catalyst as a substance that, when added to other reactants, causes a transformational energy change in them without being altered or consumed itself. In other words, a catalyst *causes* energy and transformation without *being* the transforming energy.

A simple, nonchemical analogy would be if a friend were to bring you news that you had won a lottery. That news would cause a significant reaction in you. It might even change your life. But it would not affect your friend. She (or he) would only be the catalyst, the middle person.

There are as many commonly held reasons for why humans change as there are theories about it. Freud and his followers believed that the energy that propels us into doing the things we do comes from our instinctual biological drives toward life and death.

More recent theory, including feminist theory, says that we are who we are because of our early relational experiences. New Age followers may advocate personal transformation through attitudinal healing. Others say that we are working out our karma. Astrologers base our attitudes and actions on the position of the stars and planets. Humanists tell us to look within and use the power of our own self.

All of these may have some truth to them, and many are simply saying the same thing in different images. There is an energy that we can tap into which brings about transforming change. We can find this energy directly or someone may bring it to us. When they do, they are acting as catalysts on our behalf.

As a female archetype, a catalyst is a woman in a category all her own. She is neither independent in the way the first three archetypes are, nor is she defined by her relationships, as the second three tend to be. Instead, she moves in and out of relationships, often causing incredible energy in her partner but rarely if ever committing herself to one partner over the long term. She acts very much as a midwife in that she helps to bring about new life and is intensely involved with the process, but she is not doing the birthing herself.

In the role that she does play, however, she has unique traits and strengths all her own. In the first place, the catalyst is one who attracts others. Something about her is magnetic. This is not necessarily due to her physical beauty or the force of her personality, but there is an energy or aura around her that nearly everyone can sense. This energy draws others to her. Perhaps we instinctively know that touching her in some way will cause something to happen to us, something new, creative, and exciting. We may not be sure what it is that she offers, but we know that it is there.

This may cause problems for the catalyst and those who are drawn to her. Because she does not inherently own the energy that they are seeking, she may very well not know what they want. She may assume that they are personally attracted to her as a person, whereas they are actually hoping that she will give them something they need. She is thus in constant danger of being used. The negative energies work in both directions. Her archetypal character causes *her* to make intimate connections as well. Since it is her call to transfer energy, she is drawn to touch others in a profound way.

She may not be aware of what the connection is and may be painfully misunderstood. Or she may identify it to herself as passionate love. Her partner may well respond in the same way. But the resulting relationship will be more like two wires crossing than two human energies flowing together. There will be a quick, intense burst of flame, then a rapid cooling and sizzling out. It is not difficult to translate this into a series of brief but extraordinarily intense love affairs that may leave both exhausted and confused. The energy she offers is more than sex, and it will not be physically contained.

This archetype, as all archetypes are, is one particular facet of the divine. She reflects part of God, and her energy, like that of the other archetypes, comes from God. All archetypes contain a holy calling within their being because of who they are created to be. The catalyst allows the divine energies of life, light, and love flow through her toward others. She is not the source of these energies; they come from God. But she is at least one channel or medium through which they can enter other people's lives. As she touches them with this grace, they are changed, even transformed. She is, in this way, a servant of what she carries and midwife to the new life that she helps to birth.

The catalyst will also help others believe in themselves. Her attention and personal affirmation of them will energize their own divine gifts in such a way that they may become the unique individuals that they were created to be, whichever archetypal reality they may be. To be in the presence of one of these women is a wonderful experience. She will make you feel that you are the only person in the world and that what you say, think, and feel is enormously important. This kind of affirmation produces an internal reaction that is both empowering and enabling. It does not matter that she may not remember who you are the next time she sees you. The connection made that gave you such a jolt was not between the two of you as much as it was between you and God. She only transmitted a bit of the love and affirmation that your Creator feels, and that love moved your soul.

The catalyst, then, helps to underscore the fact that the archetypes are not just psychological projections. Nor are they simply human images that reside in the collective unconscious. Rather, they are each aspects of the divine that women are given in order to give us identity, purpose, and worth. The catalyst is the one who helps us to identify these divine gifts within and who helps empower us to use them in creative ways. She brings us the Good News about ourselves, and in so doing, enables our transformation into daughters of God.

The Process

The transformation of women by God is not something evident throughout much of Scripture. In fact, fundamentalists often use biblical texts to prove that woman are not created in the divine image and are not called to anything other than to serve men. We need to note, however, that their quotations are always taken either from ancient Hebrew writings or from the Epistles. As Christians, our primary source of authority is found in neither place. It is found in the Gospels.

We look to Jesus Christ for our ultimate answers: to who he was, what he said, how he acted, what he did. And Jesus never called on woman to be subservient or inferior. Rather, he believed in women to an astonishing degree. Women were among his disciples and his closest friends. Orthodox rabbis of the first century were not allowed by law to look at, speak to, or touch a woman in public, including their mothers, wives, or daughters. There actually used to be jokes about "bleeding rabbis" who would walk into walls and doors in order to avoid being "contaminated" by women. A prayer commonly used by Jewish men declared: "Thanks be to God I was not born a woman." This is the world in which Jesus was reared. His upbringing and training would have been stringently patriarchal. As a rabbi himself, he had been well taught in these interpretations of Torah and other Hebrew Scriptures. He was a man of his times.

Yet Jesus continually blew apart all of the old edicts. He broke one law after the other, especially in regard to women. The only woman he ever reproached in the Gospels was his own mother even though he repeatedly put down his unbelieving disciples, the scribes and Pharisees, temple officials, rich men, powerful men, selfish men, thoughtless men. The fact of the matter is that if any man in history could be called a feminist, it was Jesus of Nazareth. But then, Jesus was on the side of almost any people who were treated unfairly or oppressed by others. What was more, not only was he on their side, but he said time and time again that these people were the true inheritors of God's kingdom — not the powerful or rich or strong.

No matter how hard they try, not even the most chauvinistic people can turn to the Gospels for antifeminist fuel. This is why they must use the Garden of Eden myth, the Pauline and deutero-Pauline letters, or church history. The Gospels cannot and will not be used as proof against woman's innate, inherent, God-given worth. Quite the opposite. In the Gospels, women are supported, affirmed, accepted, and even singled out for special consideration.

Here, then, is where we go to find the affirming power that the catalyst brings. She mediates the energy, but it is the power of the Holy Spirit that causes the transformational reaction.

During his lifetime, Jesus' attitudes and actions toward women were scandalously prophetic. For the most part, the Gospel writers were faithful in reporting the overwhelmingly preferential treatment Jesus afforded them. He affirmed women in every way imaginable. He broke rabbinical law by teaching them. He used women in some of his most graphic illustrations about the reign of God. He healed them from disease and emotional illness. In the Fourth Gospel, he chose to announce his messianic identity first to a Samaritan woman at a well instead of to the twelve men who were supposed to be his closest disciples. He also forgave the woman caught in adultery while at the same time implying the same degree of sin in the self-righteous men who wanted to stone her.

Jesus had many friends and disciples who were women. Aside from his mother, we are given the names of Mary Magdalene; Joanna, the wife of Herod's servant Chuza; Susanna; Mary and Martha of Bethany; Mary, the wife of Clopas; Mary, mother of James and Joses, and Salome, mother of James and John. We are told that there were some of these women and "many others, who provided for them out of their resources" (Luke 8:1–3). Obviously, many of these were well-to-do women who helped finance Jesus' ministry.

Jesus, then, came to set women free. He brought the power that would transform their lives and restore to them the divine inheritance of their Creator. In order that this restorative work continue after his death, he sent to us the Holy Spirit. As he explained to Nicodemus in decidedly feminine imagery, transformation involves being born again in the

Spirit (John 3:3). The Hebrew word for Spirit in this passage, *ruah*, which also means "wind," is feminine in grammatical gender. However, the word for Spirit in Greek is *pneuma*, grammatically neuter, and in Latin *spiritus*, grammatically masculine, so we have lost the sense of the Spirit as feminine.

Numerous examples can be cited of Jesus' restoring to women the dignity they deserve. But what is more important is the realization that his message is the one that the archetypal catalyst carries. It is Christ's energy, divine energy, that she somehow transmits. The process of transformation, however, although it is an act of God, depends to a large degree upon her comprehension of it. She is not a robot who acts in a preprogrammed way. God does not abuse us by taking away our autonomy. Instead, God teaches her through firsthand experience the message of love, acceptance, affirmation, and personal dignity that Jesus came to bring. Once she has experienced the power of this grace in her own life, she becomes a beacon that transmits it to others. This is the light, often felt as energy, to which people feel attracted in her and to which they are drawn.

Mary Magdalene

Mary of Magdala, or Mary Magdalene, is an enigmatic figure in the Gospels. Luke tells us that she was cured of seven demons (8:2). We are not, however, told either the identity of these demons or how she was healed. As to the identity of her illness, if we look at all of the other confrontations with demons in the Gospels, we find that they caused seizures (epilepsy), deafness, muteness, fever, paralysis, mental or emotional illness, and blindness. Nowhere is demon possession involved in acts of immorality, specifically sexual immorality.

Whence, then, comes the patriarchal tradition that says Mary Magdalene was a prostitute? Some say that she was the unnamed but "immoral" woman who anointed Jesus' feet with spikenard and dried them with her hair. But he did not heal that woman of seven demons; he merely forgave her sins (and in similar accounts the woman is identified as Mary of Bethany; see John 12:1–8). All we know of Mary is that she was healed, that she and other women followed Jesus, and that they helped him out of their own re-sources. In the canonical Gospels we hear no more about her until the final day of Jesus' life. It is here that the power of her faith and her love stand head and shoulders above the male disciples. Moreover, three days later the risen Christ elevates her to the position of the first apostle, the first sent out with news of the resurrection.

We are told of several women who stayed with Jesus through the terrible hours of the crucifixion: "Many women were also there, looking on from a distance; they had followed Jesus from Galilee and had provided for him. Among them were Mary Magdalene, and Mary the mother of James and Joseph, and the mother of the sons of Zebedee" (Matt. 27:55–56). Mark also tells us "there were also women looking on from a distance; among them were Mary Magdalene, and Mary the mother of James the younger and of Joses, and Salome. These used to follow him and provided for him when he was in Galilee; and there were many other women who had come up with him to Jerusalem" (Mark 15:40–41). Luke is less explicit: "But all his acquaintances, including the women who had followed him from Galilee, stood at a distance, watching these things" (Luke 23:49). John tells us that the women were closer, and that one male disciple also remained: "Meanwhile, standing near the cross of Jesus were his mother, and his mother's sister, Mary the wife of Clopas, and Mary Magdalene" (John 19:25).

Mary Magdalene is the one woman named in all three Gospels that specify who was there. Matthew and Mark put her and her companions at a distance; John adds himself and Jesus' mother to the faithful group and tells us that they were close enough to hear Jesus' last words. The point is, however, that Mary Magdalene was among the faithful, even to the end.

There are also differences in the resurrection accounts. All of the Gospels, however, describe Mary Magdalene as the first witness to the risen Lord. John's account is the most descriptive: Mary Magdalene went to the tomb alone, saw that the body was gone, and immediately went to find Peter and John. The men came to check out her story, found it to be true, and went home again. Mary stood outside the tomb, weeping (John 20:11). She saw the angels within, then, turned and "saw Jesus standing there, but she did not know that it was Jesus" (20:14). Finally, Jesus spoke directly to her:

> Jesus said to her, "Mary!" She turned and said to him in Hebrew, "Rabbouni!" (which means Teacher). Jesus said to her, "Do not hold on to me, because I have not yet ascended to the Father. But go to my brothers and say to them, `I am ascending to my Father and your Father, to my God and your God'" (John 20:16–17).

Later Jesus appeared to the others as they hid behind closed doors; then to the doubting Thomas, who had missed him the first time; and finally to Peter, who had run away completely and resumed his fishing career in Galilee.

Differences between the Gospels are always interesting, but the parallels are important as well. In all the resurrection accounts, Mary Magdalene is the first to whom the risen Lord appears — either alone or with other women. The intimacy of John's detail almost makes me want to weep. Mary calls Jesus by a personal, even endearing, word: "Rabbouni," not the formal and more proper "Rabbi." She reaches out to touch him or to be held by him. Surely, she had done so before. In all of the accounts, it is to this woman that Jesus entrusts the miraculous message, even though Jewish law forbade women to be legal witnesses.

The question that must be asked is why did Jesus choose to appear first to women? Why did he not simply appear to the twelve? And, why, above all, did he choose this particular woman?

Perhaps Jesus understands human sin much better than we give him credit for. Perhaps he knew that the disciples' pride was still a problem for them. They could not be apostles, bearers of the Good News, unless and until they had been stripped of their male ego. Had he appeared directly to them, they would have felt themselves singled out for special favor. But they were not. The special favor did not even go to his mother. That they could have understood. But this was the new order, and so Jesus chose Mary of Magdala as the first to know the enormity of God's love.

The reactions recorded in Matthew, Mark, and Luke lend credence to this theory. The men would not believe Mary or the other women. Even in John, they continued to hide behind closed doors. The reality of what had happened did not sink in. They could not accept what the women had to say. Perhaps Jesus needed to give them this one final lesson in discipleship before they were ready to be his apostles. As Paul says later in his letter to the Corinthians: "But we proclaim Christ crucified, a stumbling block to Jews and foolishness to Gentiles" (1 Cor. 1:23). Life coming from death is nonsense, no sense; it is not rational, logical, or realistic. It flies in the face of everything that masculine analysis can understand. And yet women may have a different perspective.

The Great Round

Rebirth is the central image of the Great Round. The life, death, rebirth cycle has been known and celebrated by women from earliest civilization. Women both give birth and prepare the body for burial. Women bleed and do not die but live on to bleed again. Early folk imagined Inanna and Persephone journeying to the world of the dead and returning. Earth's natural rhythms have been celebrated in feminine deities, and her lunar cycles are incarnate in woman's body. Women not only understand resurrection; we are part of it. It makes sense to us at a very profound, visceral level. We do not particularly care what theologians have to say; we do not need arguments to prove its validity; we need no lengthy explanations. We simply know its truth. It is part of our experience as women.

Perhaps this is why Jesus returned first to Mary. Above all others, she would understand. It may be that the truth of the resurrection might not have been recognized by anyone else. In fact, John says that even Mary did not know her Lord until he called her by name. The couple on the Emmaus road spent all day listening to Jesus and only in the Eucharistic meal did they realize who it was — and then Christ faded from their sight. The Good News of Jesus' resurrection can only be experienced by love and by faith. Mary, above all others, had that love and that faith. Why?

Mary Magdalene was healed of seven demons. We are not told what they were, but since seven was considered to be a complete number in biblical times, it may be assumed that this woman was sick to the very center of her soul. In this way, she is archetypical of every woman who ever lived. She bore the illnesses of us all. Then she met Jesus and was healed. We do not know whether her healing came with a word, a touch, a smile, or a look. Her healing may have been sudden, or it may have happened over the time of her discipleship. Perhaps she saw her own divine inheritance reflected back toward her in Jesus' acceptance of her as a person. Perhaps in not knowing the answers to these questions, we can all have hope for healing in our own ways.

What is clear is that Mary loved Jesus deeply and that he had special regard for her. It is also clear that because of her healing, she knew Christ's message in a sacramental, incarnational, bodily way that the men did not and could not. It was not only the words Jesus spoke or the parables Jesus told or the miracles Jesus performed. The men heard, saw, and witnessed these, too, but they could and did not receive the final message. Only Mary could accept it. She, not the twelve, had felt the power of resurrection in her own life, in her own soul.

Peter left Jerusalem and went back to Galilee to fish. Mary could never go back. She was a new person, a different person. She had been reborn. She had already experienced rebirth in her own being. Therefore, she was able to see and hear the risen Christ. It was no wonder that Jesus first reappeared to her. Jesus' final lesson to his disciples was to listen to Mary, to listen to the experience of women. Women who are catalysts are called, like Mary, to be apostles in the most profound sense of the word.

A biblical commentary from the second century and a biography of Mary of Magdala from the ninth both call her the first apostle. Two very early writings, the *Pistis Sophia* and the *Gospel of Mary Magdalene* tell us that she had, by virtue of her relationship with Jesus, her love, and her faith, a place of significant leadership in the early church. It even implies that her position was higher than that of Peter. Considering the actions of the two at the crucifixion and afterward, that would not be surprising.

Eleven of the original twelve apostles finally recognized and accepted Jesus' last lesson. They listened to the women and believed. But we also read in the gnostic *Gospel of Thomas* that the disciples were jealous of Mary because Jesus favored her over the rest. Why would he not? They never did understand what he had to say, at least not until after she brought them the news of Christ's final victory and Jesus himself followed her announcement with his own appearances and instruction.

The Twelve argued among themselves about who was the greatest and refused to listen to Jesus' words about suffering and death. Mary heard and understood it all. She stayed by him and wept for him. She did not, like the others, forsake him and flee.

Significance for Today's Woman

All of Scripture is not equal. As Christians we are to follow the Gospel of our Lord as written in Matthew, Mark, Luke, and John. The Hebrew Scriptures are an historical account of the building of a people's faith. It is the first part of the journey, the long, slow, painful climb up the mountain toward mature knowledge of God. Through the Exodus, the Law, history, wisdom literature, and the prophets, the Hebrew people struggled to know the greatness and compassion of God, but they were often mistaken.

Then Jesus came, breaking into history with the eternal word of love, the proclamation of the new reign of God. Jesus showed us signs and wonders, signal events that exemplified his message. He acted and spoke as one who knew an entirely new way to relate to self, to neighbor, and to God. He was transfigured on the mountaintop, and in his transfiguration, we were all promised transformation.

After Christ's resurrection we began the long, slow walk down the mountain. We stopped to build churches along the way as shrines to Christ's appearance. We, Paul, and others talk about what Jesus said and did, and we try to make sense of it all. We misinterpret and make mistakes, we mishear and misunderstand. Even the canonical epistles are only attempts to explain the truth that we have already seen in the person of Jesus Christ.

Christ is the one to whom we women must look for the final answers about who and what we are. In doing so, we need to look especially at Jesus' relationships with other women. Read and reread the story again. And again. And again. Women are lifted up, affirmed, accepted, healed, and encouraged. Women were taught and loved and touched. Jesus talked with women, joked with women, and debated with women. Jesus allowed women to worship and adore him with their tears and their love. With him, we have a place of honor.

Like Mary Magdalene, we have been healed of seven demons and restored to the image of God in which we were first created. Like her, we are the first recipients of the power of Christ's resurrection. By means of our love and faith, we can know Christ's message firsthand.

We too are called to be apostles. We have been commissioned in the person of Mary to speak the word of forgiveness and of new life. We have let men's charges of "whore" discourage us for too long. We need to speak to the churches, so that the churches can speak to the world. Transfiguration, transformation, is possible, but only by the power of God. We can attest to that power, but only if we accept our own healing first. If we are willing to allow the healing to happen, then we can let God's power face the consequences. And there will be consequences. Men do not like to accept a woman's word of resurrection. Even the Twelve refused to listen. But we also have Christ's word and presence behind us; we can count on that.

Mary represents the archetypal catalyst because she is one who knows the full meaning of Christ's message. She was transformed directly, by being in Christ's presence. She experienced the evil of the crucifixion and was the first to recognize life's victory in the resurrection. The Good News was more than a theological statement or an article of belief. It had quite literally become incarnate in her own being. Mary's transformation enabled her to be the first witness. It also enabled her to be the archetypal image of catalyst. She brings the message to women (as well as men) because she lived it in her life. The energy is part of her.

The healing that Mary experienced may have been from epileptic seizures or another illness, but as one who was healed, she presents us with a woman who took responsibility for her life. It was rare for Jesus to heal anyone who had not come, or at least been brought, to him. It is probably fair to assume, then, that Mary had presented herself in her illness and entrusted herself to Jesus' power.

These actions can be important for modern women. In the first place, they tell us to take the initiative when something is wrong. Our Creator does not want us to be sick: physically, mentally, emotionally, or spiritually. God always offers us relief. It is not God's intention that women be depressed, addicted, or afflicted. If we are, it is up to us to do something about it.

Part of the energy of the archetypal catalyst is this knowledge and this drive toward wholeness. She is aware at a visceral level that she, as well as others, are meant to be well. It is an important part of her power. When she looks at you and treats you as a whole, complete person, you begin to feel the wholeness that she sees. Her belief in your potential lends energy toward its fulfillment.

The power of the archetype is used internally, as well as in relationship. The catalyst is related and independent. Her energy is somewhere in us all. It can be called upon when we need a boost. She gives us our sense of being. Some call it our awareness of self. It is her voice within which tells us that deep down there is something of rare and precious beauty. She knows that we are created in God's image and will help show us the path to follow on our own particular journey to wholeness. She will then help to bring us the life, light, and love of God that will do what needs to be done.

What happened to Mary Magdalene in church history is a warning to any woman who is called to speak this kind of truth. Her announcement of the same Good News that Jesus enacted in his relationships with women will make her very threatening to those who do not want to hear. Sometime in the Middle Ages, the church decided that Mary Magdalene was a prostitute. There is no evidence to support this idea, but somehow it took hold. Today she is the patron saint of prostitutes. Actually, that may be fitting in that their victimization is not dissimilar. But this is what any woman will be called if she emits the kind of energy that Mary Magdalene did and still does.

Mary obviously did not care what others thought, an attitude that people are not accustomed to seeing in a woman. She had no fear of what the authorities would do to her as a mourner at the foot of the cross or as a solitary visitor to the tomb. She simply did what love bade her do. The catalyst will act in the same way. She will not care about the opinion of others, and she will act independently of consequences. That may cause her problems, and she may be considered socially unacceptable because of it, but it may simply be that she knows a larger truth that sets her free from worrying about appearances.

The catalytic process, then, is one of healing or transformation, of resurrection. Mary Magdalene is a witness to us of this great possibility. She was asked to pass it on. The archetypal catalyst of today is also called to keep the power of resurrection alive by witnessing to its reality. She need not do this in words. Others will see it in her eyes, her face, her actions. She will emanate a radiance or a glow to which others are drawn. People will say that there is a "presence" about her that they cannot describe but that they enjoy. They feel whole when they are with her.

To witness from one's own being is a call that may seem threatening, but one that is enormously empowering to others. Women have always shared their vulnerabilities more than men and have enjoyed hearing one another's stories. Now we are gathering together very intentionally in order to share the experiences we have been through. Sometimes, all that is heard is the pain and frustration of abuse. At other times the story is one of desperate seeking for answers that never seem to be found.

But there are other women who are archetypal catalysts such as Mary Magdalene. Their personal stories have an energy from beyond themselves. They point to a force much greater than themselves, a force that somehow has made itself present in their lives. They share incredible experiences of healing and forgiveness, love and acceptance. In hearing the stories, others are empowered. The same energy, divine energy, that touched them, touches those who hear. This is the catalyst's gift and her call. Listen to her voice in other women and in yourself. Celebrate the wholeness that is there. Allow and invite the transformation to begin.

Questions for Reflection

The most important aspect of the catalyst is her recognition, in others and in ourselves. These questions may help. After meditating a while on them, try the visualizations that follow.

1. *Has there been resurrection in your life? When? How? Who were the catalysts?*

2. *Has anyone had more faith in you than you have had in yourself? What happened?*

3. *Have you been able to hear the voice within that tells you of your beauty and worth? If not, how can you take the time to listen?*

4. *What would your life be like if you accepted that you are created in the image of God?*

Now allow yourself to enter into the Gospel of John's account of the resurrection. Take Mary's place as she walks through the wet grass in the very early hours of the new day. Feel her despair and grief as she nears the place where Jesus' bleeding body had been hastily laid. Imagine her shock at seeing the stone moved away and the tomb empty.

What are your thoughts? What would you do? Can you sense the presence of the two angels standing where the body had lain? Now let your awareness turn to the one who appears behind you. He looks familiar, but your mind is reeling and your sorrow too great to think. Has he taken your friend, your love, your Lord? He looks at your face, then reaches out to you, and speaks your name. . . .

Now envision yourself in a place of incredible natural beauty, your very favorite place in the universe. You are standing on the earth with a bright, blue sky overhead. All of nature is alive with buzzing, singing, darting energy and joy. Enjoy the beauty of creation all around you. Feel yourself a part of it. Then let yourself slowly become aware of someone else with you. Look slowly around. Whom do you see? A person in comfortable clothes, a person who is not terribly attractive, but the face! Look at that face — and especially the eyes. See the love shining back at you, looking into the center of your being. You are known as fully as you can be known... and you are accepted as you are. You are affirmed. You are loved. You are healed. You are whole.

PART
FIVE

IMAGE

CHAPTER NINE

Where Do We Go from Here?

In the second volume of Jung's *Collected Works* (1958), he makes what is truly a remarkable statement for a psychologist:

> Among all my patients in the second half of life — that is to say, over 35 — there has not been one whose problem in the last resort was not that of finding a religious outlook on life. It is safe to say, that every one of them fell ill because he [she] had lost what the living religions of every age have given their followers, and none of them has been really healed who did not regain his [her] religious perspective (p. 334).

Where do we go from here? For many women, we go back to the roots of our faith. The archetypes that we have met each represent an aspect of the divine being. As women we can readily accept at least one or two of them as active in our lives, even if we have not recognized them before as a gift from God. Perhaps this new awareness will help us to embrace their reality a little more readily. Psychologically speaking, they help us to know better the strengths and weaknesses of our own being. Theologically speaking, they help us interact more freely with our Creator, and to appropriate the affirmation and worth that God offers to us through them. But beyond these important aspects, the biblical archetypes help us understand what we are called to do in the world around us.

Knowing Ourselves

Archetype is a psychological term. Jung and his followers saw them as conceptual realities that live deeply within the collective unconscious of every human being. In a very real way, they tie us all together with their universality. They also provide us with energy. We innately seem to behave as if one or more of them were directing us in their own particular way. To one familiar with archetypal images, women can be identified by their names, but the power of archetypes is more than simple identification. Getting to know them in terms of representational images helps us to name our strengths and beware of our weaknesses. In terms of energy, we can appropriate the positive forces of the archetype and decide what action to take with or against the negative.

Archetypes, as energy, are not static. They develop and change over the course of one's lifetime. They can also change over the course of a single day. Within one woman, the archetypal mother may see her kids off to school, the sister goes to work as a counselor in a women's crisis center, the daughter stops by her mother's on the way home, the wife prepares her husband's meal, the wise one listens to her teenager's concerns about growing up, and the catalyst makes passionate love before falling asleep. Meanwhile, the fathers' daughter is planning their financial future in such a way that the kids can go to college without bankrupting the rest of the family. And yet this is all the same woman.

Developing the strengths of each archetype will help her through the day. She can count on the archetypes to fully enjoy the tasks they are given to do, and all her various roles will be fulfilling. But she needs to be careful to let only one lead at a time. The mother may thoroughly enjoy getting the kids off to school, but the sister might be frustrated by their slowness and be eager to get rid of them so that she can go to work. The sister will be a dynamite counselor, but the daughter may be hooked by an older supervisor who deals harshly with her. The daughter will enjoy visiting her mother after work, but the wife may feel guilty about not being home when her husband arrives. The wife may fix a delicious meal but ignore the needs of her teen. The catalyst will have a wonderful time in bed, but the mother may worry that the kids can hear. The fathers' daughter may drive everyone crazy figuring out more and more ways to save money. The wise one will wonder what all the activity is about and ask them all to slow down and smell the roses.

One of the most difficult challenges any modern woman faces is her changing roles. The example above is hardly unusual; life may be much more complex than that. It is therefore extremely important to know which archetype to call on at a particular time. We are no good as a mother if our sister archetype is impatient, and so on. Keeping them straight also helps prevent the devastating sickness of guilt. The three relational archetypes are particularly susceptible if they cannot be objective about their own reality.

For example, an archetypal wife may feel that she ought to do all the housework, but she is also working, parenting, and trying to find time for herself. If she can switch into a more independent mode, she can more easily look at her situation and see the validity of her own needs, thereby diffusing the guilt. How does she do that? It may be no more difficult than taking some time to sit down and consciously put herself in the mode of the wise one. She can then allow the guilty one to speak to her and listen to her wisdom. Or she may ask the catalyst to empower the independent ones with strength so that their demands will be accepted as just.

Archetypes also change over the long term. I have asked many women to share their journeys with me in relation to the archetypes, and every one of them saw shifts over the years. One of the most difficult shifts is the shift from relational to independent archetypes. Several women acknowledged the first stage of the archetypal daughter through school and into their first job. They were then married and became the archetypal wife, putting their partners above all else. Then the kids came along, and they identified most strongly with the mother. But after ten years or so, midlife hit, and a whole new set of priorities and energies emerged. Frequently, they felt the power of the sister for the first time, which caused chaos! For several women, it meant the end of their marriage and a switch in career. Understanding the archetypal energy that was pushing them helped these women to see what had happened and why. Other women who had been living out of an independent archetype all their lives suddenly began to yearn for spouse and children.

The situations all vary, and in each case the women needed to deal with both the positive and the negative forces as the archetypes took leadership positions within their souls. But looking back, they found meaning in each archetypal image as they became acquainted with them.

In God's Image

Psychology, as helpful as it may be, is not enough. Some women can find a sense of validation, integrity, and worth within themselves. They are the fortunate ones. They object strenuously to the idea that we might go anywhere else to get it. In one way, they are right. We do not need to go to our parents, our spouses, our children, or the social order for affirmation of who we are as women. That knowledge *is* within us, but it is a knowledge that is *given* to us.

Just as we are endowed with the genetic imprint of God, we are also given that innate knowledge of our own integrity. Because our archetypal reality is one facet of the divine light, we, too, are holy and have eternal worth. No matter how we might misuse or misrepresent the reality we have been given, it is never retracted. Once the Creator's image has been bestowed, it is never taken away. It may be covered up, distorted, or used negatively, as Herodias, Delilah, Jezebel, and other biblical women illustrate. Yet their reality was still of blessing and of God, and no matter what they did with their lives, the center of their being remained part of that holy image.

It is therefore true that we do not need to go beyond ourselves for a sense of validation and worth; we need to also accept that blessing as a divine gift from the God in whose image we are shaped. It is not ourselves that we worship; we are not the Creator. We merely help in the creative process by utilizing our gifts in constructive ways and by aligning ourselves with the intentions of God in the world.

Using Our Gifts

As important as it is to know who we are and to be able to accept our God-given worth, we need also to ask the question "Why?" For what purpose are we given such a holy gift?

The seekers of the Holy Grail were challenged to ask the question, "Whom does it serve?" It is a legitimate concern. It is not enough to appreciate our beauty and worth as women. We also have a task to do. God has work to accomplish in the world, and we are each to do our part. Being created in the divine image is not solely a matter of personal validation. It also means that God's intent for the healing, justice, and peace of creation is our business as well.

As a geosphere we face very real and potentially disastrous problems. Economic thunderheads are rising that could shake the Western world to its foundations. The rapid expansion of so-called Third World countries will soon threaten our cherished caucasian isolationism. Our country faces difficulties in government that it has never faced before, and regardless of the political rhetoric, no one has any answers.

We, as women, live in a time unlike any other. We have to accept our own responsibilities — financial, political, and legal, as well as psychological. We need to exercise leadership in these areas as we have never done before. The issues that need to be addressed in this world are potentially devastating. Environmental issues alone are enough for several generations of women to concentrate on full time in order to make even a dent in the mess we have made of our world. Global hunger and drought are spreading as we continue to disrupt the food chain. Oppression of people of color, of the old and the very young, of the illiterate, and of the poor are endemic. Phobias against people of different sexual orientation cause exclusion and even violence. The AIDS epidemic pulls people apart in hatred rather than bringing them together in compassion.

In addition to these seemingly overwhelming global concerns, families in this country need medical care, child care, and afford-able housing. Women are in danger of losing reproductive rights over their own bodies. Mothers need to be paid fairly for what they do. Both parents need flexible schedules to accommodate their children's needs. Families need health insurance and affordable car insurance. Senior citizens need help with the overwhelming costs of hospital stays and nursing care. People need banks in which their hard-earned savings are secure. The issues go on and on. Competition must give way to cooperation; fighting must give way to affiliation; and caring for one another has become necessary for our very existence. Survival as a planet and a people depend on a reordering of our values.

Women know a better way. We know it instinctively and intu-itively. We have always been able to make hard choices in order to help others, but too often we did it at our own expense. Now, however, we can make the hard choices out of our own archetypal strengths and not destroy our integrity in the process. We can no longer allow other people to define our reality for us. We need not even turn to psychology to explain how we got to be this way and how to accept our supposed shortcomings. Nor are we obligated to listen to biblical quotations from patriarchal churches that "prove" our inherent inequality and supposed God-given inferiority. There is a better way.

But it does not mean turning our backs on all we love and cherish, either, including men, children, and the church. Nor does it mean, as we thought it did in the 1970s, that we are to go out and seek a new identity. Rather, we can learn to make the hard choices ahead based on the identity that was ours in the very beginning. Psychology has been very helpful and useful in sorting out some of our early misconceptions, but it cannot give us that crucial, fundamental sense of our own worth that we yearn for so desperately. That issue, as Carl Jung says, is inherently a question of religion, of faith.

Putting It All Together

The Judeo-Christian faith is not quite as misogynist as it may appear. It is clear now, given modern critical methods of biblical interpretation, that Scripture has always said that women are created in the image of God. The first two chapters of Genesis have been grossly misread for millenia in order to document what patriarchal society deemed to be "right." Women have, by and large, accepted the verdict. To do otherwise would have meant conflict and responsibility, which we were taught to avoid. In other words, we took the easy road. Or at least, it seemed to be the easy road.

Now, however, women are utilizing the archetypal strengths we have been given as part of the divine image to help in God's work in the world. Some of us will work within the established order, along with Ruth and Naomi. We will work within present institutions and old-boy networks, using to full advantage the strategic intelligence with which we have been blessed. But we will beware that we do not merely use our gifts to gain personal power, like Herodias. Nor should we use our feminine beauty and sensuality as a lure and a weapon. We fathers' daughters have exceptional gifts to use: gifts of intelligence and administration. We can accomplish much because we will not demand systemic change. We can use the system as it is and still accomplish whatever we set our minds on achieving. We are women of power and can use that power creatively and constructively toward the important issues that we face.

Judith, on the other hand, is a woman's woman. She represents those of us who are more comfortable working outside patriarchal systems of power. Basically independent and goal-directed, we tend to rely on the help of other women. We can begin to design new ways of doing things. Like Judith, we can refuse to be conquered and work out our own ways of defeating oppressive forces. Working with other women, we can free society from the patriarchal bonds with which it has been bound. But we will have to be aware of our negative potential as well. Judith may have been on the right side, but some of her techniques were less than honorable. We will need to be careful that our love of justice does not become violent, even against oppressors. Our deepest shadow may include Delilah, the negative energy in every feminist's soul who would emasculate men and strip them violently of their patriarchal power. Revenge is an understandable reaction on the part of any victim against her oppressor, but we are called upon to build a new way, not to be as destructive as the old.

Huldah is the wise, warm, wonderful woman who sits patiently within our soul waiting for us to come to her. When we become involved with our families, careers, and relationships, whether our issues and agendas are Ruth's or Judith's, we will need to check in with Huldah on a regular basis in order to remain centered. She is critical to our growth and our ability to move into the new responsibilities to which we are called. Without her, we are at risk of falling prey to our negative side. Huldah will wait for us to call. Remember, it was not she who sought the king; Josiah went to her.

This is the source of feminine wisdom to which even men and governments must eventually turn, not because women are better than men, but because, as Jung has pointed out so clearly, it is the feminine that leads men to their own spiritual center. The wise one is the guide who can and who will lead to God. Once she speaks, she must be obeyed. Huldah's gift was not only in translating the present but in discerning the past and predicting its effects upon the future. She then cushioned the harshest words in compassion. We need to hear her voice today. Not only in terms of justice and peace but particularly in terms of the ecosystem, we need to look honestly at our past actions, name our sins of the present, and courageously face the realities of the future. Hopefully, we have not gone too far in our own destruction.

The center of our focus, though, must be the imago Dei. Out of this, Ruth and Judith receive and obey their call. Out of this, Huldah speaks with the voice and the wisdom of God. The earth creature is our primal image: *ha-adam*, a being both female and male, both feminine and masculine, as is our Creator. This primal image represents the wholeness in our own soul that Jung identifies as the "Self." It also represents the God-given plan for all of creation. With the creation of *ish* and *ishshah*, God did not intend separation, division, or competition. God constructed no hierarchy within creation. All of creation was intended to be a single entity, one in itself and one with the Creator. This is the eschatological image of the peaceable kingdom when wild animals and little children can play together in harmony. Perhaps lions and babies are easier to imagine at peace than male and female, husband and wife. And yet, that is our inheritance and that is our promise. It is also our reality, given to us at the moment of our conception. The divine image is no less.

The mother and the daughter are archetypal images to which all women react. Psychology has impressed upon us the overwhelming power of mothers' impact upon our being. How many of us continue to live out our lives under our mothers' shadows? Either we endlessly seek their approval, or we spend our days defiantly proving our independence.

As mothers, too, we have taken our power to heart. We do all we can to see that our children are "raised right." We want to bring them up to be successful, happy, stable, intelligent, strong. And when they are rich and famous, we want to hear them turn from the roaring crowds toward the cameras and say, "Thanks, Mom!" We do give ourselves a rather monumental task! And we willingly accept the blame when all does not go as planned. If only we had sacrificed more!

Sarah, Isaac's mother, provides us with the archetypal image of who we think we are meant to be: obedient, humble, self-sacrificing, loyal, faithful. But look at the story again: Sarai obeyed Abram and went to Pharaoh, and God said, "No!" Sarai gave Hagar to Abram to conceive the child she so desperately wanted, and God said, "No!" She obeyed Abram again and became part of Abimelech's harem, and once again God said, "No!" Finally, Sarah heard the message from the angels herself. God then said, "Yes," and she conceived. Her son was named by her only honest emotion in the story: laughter. Finally, in saving Isaac, God put to rest forever the kind of self-sacrifice that Sarah had thought was divine will. For a final time, God said, "No!"

Mothers are not called upon to destroy themselves on behalf of their children. Created in God's image, we are instead called upon to realize that divine inheritance in ourselves. As for our children, our greatest task is to see that they accept responsibility for growing into their own God-given selves. And they must do this by themselves; we cannot and are not to do it for them. Our call as mothers, then, may sound very new, but it is as old as Scripture. We need to back off and let God lead.

Nowhere is this more evident than in the story of Mary of Nazareth. As archetypal image of a woman who grows from daughter into mature wisdom, she provides the role model of a woman who had to let go of both parents and child(ren) in order to grow into God's image. Her success as Jesus' mother was not in providing him with a stable, comfortable home so that he would provide for her in her old age. Her success came in finally learning that he must follow his own call, even though it meant losing him completely. In what must have looked to all observers like defeat, Jesus named in Mary and John a whole new and wonderful identification of motherhood and family.

The family is important to the structure of society. The problem has been that it has too often been identified only in terms of the nuclear family: that is, patriarchal Dad in charge, Mom at home in the kitchen, kids at school and play. It has too often been exclusive and self-centered, interested only in its own preservation and security, comfort and success.

That is not Jesus' understanding of either family or church. If we are to take responsibility in this new age, we need to redefine these very basic images. Jesus taught us that his family was not biologically determined but centered in faith. Mary learned that her son belonged to the whole world and not only to her. John heard that he was responsible not only for his mother Salome but also for other widows. The early church was very clear on this. They cared for one another as sisters and brothers in Christ.

Jesus would take us one step further. Not only is the church responsible for its own; it is also responsible for teaching the whole world about the familial love of the Abba. If we lived the love that the Gospels teach, we could really begin to make a dent against the deadly oppressions and injustices of the world. If women began to insist upon feeding the hungry children on the streets and around the world, freeing our brothers and sisters from the endless cycle of poverty, and providing homes, food, and medical care to our parents across the nation, there might be a rethinking of priorities.

Mary learned to accept a universal outlook upon humanity that was evidenced in the apostolic surge of the early church. Beginning as a naive child, she accepted the responsibility of journeying through hell in order to come out on the side of life. We may be asked to do the same.

Finally, we speak of healing and transformation. In fact, we have been speaking of little else. Like Mary Magdalene, we women have been given a message to deliver. People may not want to hear it and may refuse to believe it, but we have been given a task to perform and fidelity means that we must do it.

First of all, we have a message to one another as women. By Jesus' words and actions, women were restored to their rightful place in the imago Dei. We have been affirmed by Christ and entrusted with the Good News of Christ's resurrection. Like Mary, we have been healed of the demons set upon us by history. Like her, we are not required to be wives or mothers in order to "win approval." We are loved as the faithful people that we are.

Second, Jesus told us to tell the men to go to Galilee and wait for him there. What does that mean today? It means that men are to be attentive to what we have to say as women. It means that men are to leave "Jerusalem," the center of wealth and power, and turn their time and attention to the creation that we are rapidly destroying. It means that men are to give up their need for control and allow the Christ Spirit to redirect their lives.

Finally, we have a message to the churches. For too long, we have used the cross to batter, bruise, and oppress. So-called Christians have murdered and tortured, waged wars and crusades, instigated bloody inquisitions and pogroms, even legalized slavery and apartheid on the basis of "God's will." Today, if Jesus saw our ornate church buildings with the homeless huddled on grates in front of them while million-dollar budgets are spent on maintenance and repair and church leaders bicker about status and position, he would weep in frustration and pain. Maybe it is time for the tables of the temple to be overturned again.

We have gotten badly off track, and it is time to get back on. We are destroying our earth, our beautiful garden. We are polluting ourselves and poisoning our children. We are letting people starve while we build more missiles, bombs, and chemical weapons. Like the bleeding rabbis, we will not see those whom we wish to avoid: the homeless, the homosexual, the alcoholic, the person with AIDS, the addict, the starving, the abused. Our human family lies in the dirt with bloated bellies and biting flies, waiting for a healing touch. Who will bring it to them if we will not?

We are Naomi and Ruth, Judith and Huldah, *ishshah* and Sarah, Mary of Nazareth and Mary Magdalene — persons created in God's image, healed by God, and given God's message of transformation and hope. We have the strengths of all these women.

What is more, we know resurrection. We have witnessed it; we have experienced it in our lives. Now it is time to be whom God created us to be, to speak and to act. By God's grace, let us begin.

Bibliography

Achtemeir, Elizabeth. *The Committed Marriage*. Philadelphia: Westminster Press, 1976.

Baigent, Leigh and Lincoln. *Holy Blood, Holy Grail*. New York: Dell Publishing Co., 1983.

Bankson, Marjory. *Braided Streams*. San Diego: LuraMedia, 1985.

————. *Seasons of Friendship*. San Diego: LuraMedia, 1987.

Barnhouse, Ruth T. *Identity*. Philadelphia: Westminster Press, 1984.

Bolen, Jean S. *Goddesses in Everywoman: A New Psychology of Women*. New York: Harper & Row, 1984.

Brownmiller, Susan. *Femininity*. New York: Fawcett Columbine, 1984.

Caplan, Paula. *The Myth of Women's Masochism*. New York: E. P. Dutton, 1985.

Castillejo, Irene. *Knowing Woman: A Feminine Psychology*. New York: Harper & Row, 1973.

Chesler, Phyllis. *Mothers on Trial*. New York: McGraw-Hill, 1986.

Daly, Mary. *Pure Lust: Elemental Feminist Psychology.* Boston: Beacon Press, 1984.

Deen, Edith. *All of the Women of the Bible.* New York: Harper & Row, 1983.

Diehl, Judith R. *A Woman's Place.* Philadelphia: Fortress Press, 1985.

Dowling, Colette. *The Cinderella Complex.* New York: Pocket Books, 1981.

Duerk, Judith. *Circle of Stones.* San Diego: LuraMedia, 1987.

Eichenbaum, Luise, and Susie Orbach. *Understanding Women: A Feminist Psycho-analytic Approach.* New York: Basic Books, 1983.

Emswiler, Sharon. *The On-going Journey: Women and the Bible.* New York: Women's Division, General Board of Global Ministries, The United Methodist Church, 1977.

Erikson, Erik. *Childhood and Society.* New York: W. W. Norton & Co., 1950, 1963.

Fiorenza, Elisabeth Schussler. *In Memory of Her.* New York: Crossroad, 1985.

French, Marilyn. *Beyond Power: On Women, Men and Morals.* New York: Ballantine Books, 1985.

Friedan, Betty. *The Second Stage.* New York: Summit Books, 1981, 1986.

Gilligan, Carol. *In a Different Voice.* Cambridge, MA: Harvard University Press, 1982.

Greenberg, Jay R., and Stephen A. Mitchell. *Object Relations in Psychoanalytic Theory.* Cambridge, MA: Harvard University Press, 1983.

Greenspan, Miriam. *A New Approach to Women and Therapy.* New York: McGraw-Hill, 1983.

Horney, Karen. *Feminine Psychology.* New York: W. W. Norton & Co., 1939.

Hosmer, Rachel. *Gender and God: Love and Desire in Christian Spirituality.* New York: Cowley Publications, 1986.

Jewett, Paul. *MAN as Male and Female.* Grand Rapids, MI: Eerdmans, 1975.

Johnson, Robert. *She: Understanding Feminine Psychology.* New York: Harper & Row, 1976.

Joy, Donald and Robbie. *Lovers — Whatever Happened to Eden?* Waco, TX: Word Books, 1987.

Jung, Carl G. *Man and His Symbols.* New York: Dell Publishing Co., 1964.

Kalven, Janet, and Mary I. Buckley. *Women's Spirit Bonding*. New York: Pilgrim Press, 1984.

Kegan, Robert. *The Evolving Self*. Cambridge, MA: Harvard University Press, 1982.

Leonard, Linda. *The Wounded Woman*. Boulder, CO: Shambhala Publications, 1982.

Loder, Ted. *Eavesdropping on the Echoes*. San Diego: LuraMedia, 1987.

Marshall, Megan. *The Cost of Loving: Women and the New Fear of Intimacy*. New York: G. P. Putnam's Sons, 1984.

Mattoon, Mary Ann. *Jungian Psychology in Perspective*. New York: The Free Press, Macmillan Publishing Co., 1981.

Miller, Jean Baker. *Toward a New Psychology of Women*. Boston: Beacon Press, 1976.

Mollenkott, Virginia Ramey. *The Divine Feminine*. New York: Crossroad, 1983.

Mowbray, Carol T., Susan Lanir, and Marilyn Hulce, eds. *Women and Mental Health: New Directions for Change*. New York: Harrington Park Press, 1985.

Neumann, Erich. *The Origins and History of Consciousness*. Princeton, NJ: Princeton University Press, 1954.

Norwood, Robin. *Women Who Love Too Much*. New York: Pocket Books, 1986.

Nunnally-Cox, Janice. *Foremothers*. New York: Seabury Press, 1981.

Payne, Dorothy. *Singleness*. Philadelphia: Westminster Press, 1983.

Peck, Jane Cary. *Self and Family*. Philadelphia: Westminster Press, 1984.

Perera, Sylvia. *Descent to the Goddess*. Toronto: Inner City Books, 1981.

Rollins, Wayne G. *Jung and the Bible*. Atlanta: John Knox Press, 1983.

Russell, Letty. *Growth in Partnership*. Philadelphia: Westminster Press, 1981.

———. *Becoming Human*. Philadelphia: Westminster Press, 1982.

Sanford, John. *The Invisible Partners*. New York: Paulist Press, 1980.

Schaef, Anne Wilson. *Women's Reality*. Minneapolis: Winston Press, 1981.

Shainess, Natalie. *Sweet Suffering*. New York: Pocket Books, 1984.

Soelle, Dorothy. *The Strength of the Weak*. Philadelphia: Westminster Press, 1984.

Spretnak, Charlene. *Lost Goddesses of Early Greece*. Boston: Beacon Press, 1978.

Stone, Merlin. *When God Was a Woman*. New York: Harcourt, Brace, Jovanovich, 1976.

Trible, Phyllis. *God and the Rhetoric of Sexuality*. Philadelphia: Fortress Press, 1978.

Ulanov, Ann Belford. *Receiving Woman*. Philadelphia: Westminster Press, 1981.

Weidman, Judith, ed. *Christian Feminism*. San Francisco: Harper & Row, 1984.

Whitmont, Edward C. *Return of the Goddess*. New York: Crossroad, 1986.

Woodman, Marion. *Addiction to Perfection*. Toronto: Inner City Books, 1982.

Craig Ballard Millett

A graduate of Colby College in Waterville, Maine, Craig received her master of divinity and doctor of ministry degrees from Andover Newton Theological School, Newton Centre, Massachusetts.

For several years she served as chaplain at Andover Newton and taught courses in psychology, women's studies, spiritual growth, and Christian healing. She is the mother of three daughters.

Ordained in the United Church of Christ, Craig and her husband are now involved in a church planting ministry near Orlando, Florida.

LuraMedia Publications

Marjory Zoet Bankson, BRAIDED STREAMS: Esther and a Woman's Way of Growing *(ISBN 0-931055-05-09)*

SEASONS OF FRIENDSHIP: Naomi and Ruth as a Pattern *(ISBN 0-931055-41-5)*

Carolyn Stahl Bohler, PRAYER ON WINGS: A Search for Authentic Prayer *(ISBN 0-931055-72-5)*

Alla Renée Bozarth, WOMANPRIEST: A Personal Odyssey *(ISBN 0-931055-51-2)*

Mary Cartledge-Hays, TO LOVE DELILAH: Claiming the Women of the Bible *(ISBN 0-931055-68-7)*

Judy Dahl, RIVER OF PROMISE: Two Women's Story of Love and Adoption *(ISBN 0-931055-64-4)*

Judith Duerk, CIRCLE OF STONES: Woman's Journey to Herself *(ISBN 0-931055-66-0)*

Lura Jane Geiger and Patricia Backman, BRAIDED STREAMS: Leader's Guide *(ISBN 0-931055-09-1)*

Lura Jane Geiger and Susan Tobias, SEASONS OF FRIENDSHIP: Leader's Guide *(ISBN 0-931055-74-1)*

Lura Jane Geiger, Sandy Landstedt, Mary Geckeler and Peggie Oury, ASTONISH ME, YAHWEH!: A Bible Workbook-Journal *(ISBN 0-931055-01-6)*

Kenneth L. Gibble, THE GROACHER FILE: A Satirical Exposé of Detours to Faith *(ISBN 0-931055-55-5)*

Ronna Fay Jevne, Ph.D. and Alexander Levitan, M.D., NO TIME FOR NONSENSE: Self-Help for the Seriously and Chronically Ill *(ISBN 0-931055-63-6)*

Ted Loder, EAVESDROPPING ON THE ECHOES: Voices from the Old Testament *(ISBN 0-931055-42-3 HB; ISBN 0-931055-58-X PB)*

GUERRILLAS OF GRACE: Prayers for the Battle *(ISBN 0-931055-04-0)*

NO ONE BUT US: Personal Reflections on Public Sanctuary *(ISBN 0-931055-08-3)*

TRACKS IN THE STRAW: Tales Spun from the Manger *(ISBN 0-931055-06-7)*

Joseph J. Luciani, Ph.D., HEALING YOUR HABITS: Introducing Directed Imagination, a Successful Technique for Overcoming Addictive Problems *(ISBN 0-931055-71-7)*

Jacqueline McMakin with Sonya Dyer, WORKING FROM THE HEART: For Those Who Hunger for Meaning and Satisfaction in Their Work *(ISBN 0-931055-65-2)*

Richard C. Meyer, ONE ANOTHERING: Biblical Building Blocks for Small Groups *(0-931055-73-3)*

Elizabeth O'Connor, SEARCH FOR SILENCE, Revised Edition *(ISBN 0-931055-07-5)*

Donna Schaper, A BOOK OF COMMON POWER: Narratives Against the Current *(ISBN 0-931055-67-9)*

SUPERWOMAN TURNS 40: The Story of One Woman's Intentions to Grow Up *(ISBN 0-931055-57-1)*

Renita Weems, JUST A SISTER AWAY: A Womanist Vision of Women's Relationships in the Bible *(ISBN 0-931055-52-0)*

LuraMedia is a company that searches for ways to encourage personal growth, shares the excitement of creative integrity, and believes in the power of faith to change lives.

7060 Miramar Rd., Suite 104
San Diego, California 92121